DRACULA'S
WHITBY

DRACULA'S
WHITBY

Ian Thompson

AMBERLEY

First published 2012

Amberley Publishing
The Hill, Stroud
Gloucestershire, GL5 4EP

www.amberleybooks.com

British Library Cataloguing in Publication Data.
A catalogue record for this book is available from the British Library.

ISBN 978 1 4456 0288 2

Typesetting and Origination by Amberley Publishing.
Printed in Great Britain.

Contents

Acknowledgements

I would like to thank the following people for their assistance in making this book possible: Roger Frost for steering me in the right direction time and time again, as well as offering valuable advice; all the staff at the Whitby Archives for allowing me to view the original *Whitby Gazettes* from 1890; and Bram Stoker, without whom none of this would have happened.

Behold the dark, holier and more gracious than thy Black shroud.
Beneath the cool flame of lust, rigor mortis of thy soul falls emancipated from your brow.
Confide languidly amongst the spy glass whilst the clad procession passes by to emerge metamorphasised and yet held against the blackest will.
Your fate is as was told to be and your angel's wings cast aside their disguise.
For you are one of darkness, an innocent child born of a wicked sinful place.
A place where a shadow has no form to follow.

'Behold The Dark'
Melanie Wall
1993

Introduction

Welcome to Whitby.

You are no doubt reading this because you know that Whitby is connected to the Dracula story and you want to know how the world's most famous vampire is linked to a North Yorkshire fishing town.

As a child I was spellbound by horror films and scary stories, staying up late (often in secret, with the television volume turned low and a pillow pressed against the bottom of the door to disguise the tell-tale blue flicker from passing parents) to watch Hammer Horror films, and to revel in lurid vampire adventures, often featuring the infamous Count Dracula. I read stories about vampires and monsters in comics, re-read the same books in the library about ghosts and witches, and even drew eerie creatures on scraps of paper I found lying about the house. My best friend from school was a girl who lived just around the corner from me and was just as obsessed, if not more, than I was. After a particularly creepy film had been on television in the middle of the night, Melanie and I would then meet in the school playground the following day to discuss the cinematic monsters, recounting the tales of horror and gore, and arguing about whether or not the hero should have won. We would make up lurid vampire stories to scare our classmates, often receiving stern words from our teachers for upsetting the other children. I remember being sent to the headmaster's office for reducing a younger child to tears, all because I told him that there was a werewolf living in the woods near his house!

Then, whilst recovering from a hospital stay at the tender age of eight, my mother bought me a *Classics Illustrated* graphic novel. These books were picture strips of all the great classics of literature, designed to encourage younger readers to broaden their minds and possibly try their hand at reading the original. One of these *Classics Illustrated*, the one my mother bought for me, was an adaptation of the Dracula story and I was quickly hooked! The graphic novel was far better than anything I had seen on television, with its fantastic artwork and captivating story. Within a year I had borrowed Bram Stoker's *Dracula* from the local library and quickly read it.

My mother comes from Whitby and it didn't take long for me to make the connection between the North Yorkshire seaside town that I had often visited and my favourite horror story. Every trip to Whitby from then on became a pilgrimage and I would visit each of the locations from the story, often running up the 199 steps to the churchyard or peeking up narrow alleyways during the summer evenings to see if I could spot bats flitting about and, when I did, wondering if they were actually vampires looking for victims.

Now I'm older but my enthusiasm for *Dracula* and Whitby remains as strong as ever. I make sure I visit Whitby at least once a year. The mystique of the ultimate vampire legend still holds me in its grip like no other story can. Indeed, I have not yet read a vampire story that comes close to *Dracula*.

I think that it is fair to say that Dracula – the vampire – is the most archetypal of all vampires in literature and the arts. You only have to mention the name 'Dracula' and an image will instantly pop into your head. And most people have a very strong personal image of Dracula, no doubt created by their own particular experiences of the story. He may look aristocratic, dressed in white tie and tails as portrayed by the actor Bela Lugosi. He may be tall and bear more than a passing resemblance to Christopher Lee. Perhaps he looks more like Gary Oldman? I suppose it all depends on which films you were first introduced to. It is worth noting, at this point, that Dracula has been portrayed by more actors than any other character within the horror genre, so you would have plenty of different interpretations to choose from!

Personally, I was captivated by the 1979 Universal film featuring Frank Langella and directed by John Badham. With its overt references to Whitby and some very sinister vampires and characters, it really stuck in my mind and still remains one of my favourite vampire films of all time. My fondness of this particular film is further reinforced by the fact that, as a child growing up in Cornwall, my family would often take trips to the beach at Carlyon Bay. There I would play for hours on what appeared to be the wreck of a small wooden ship, half buried in the fine sand. This wreck was, in fact, the remains of the set of the schooner that brought Dracula to England from my favourite film.

Dracula is such an iconic figure that he has inspired hundreds of films and television programmes. In fact he has appeared in over 215 films and, since its publication in 1897, *Dracula* has never been out of print – surely a sign of immortality!

As we move into more recent years, 'Goths' – followers of a particular genre of music and literature – have discovered Whitby and it has become the venue for the world-famous Whitby Goth Weekends, held twice a year. Inspired in part by Gothic Horror, the Goth style has now evolved into a punk-like fashion, but the pilgrimage that so many of these amazing people make to Whitby is, without a doubt, a nod to the town's *Dracula* connections and the Count's status within the Goth culture.

In 1997, the centenary of the publication of Stoker's novel was celebrated at the Metropole Hotel in Whitby. Dracula enthusiasts from all over the country just had to be there – myself and my best friend Richard included. The Goths were there, as were the die-hard Dracula fans, wearing fangs and long black cloaks. Also present were those who take their inspiration from the films and novels of Anne Rice.

The presence of the fantastic Hammer Horror actress Ingrid Pitt (a familiar face to me since childhood, and far better in the flesh!) made the event simply perfect for many. Sadly, Ingrid died recently but I will always remember her as a wonderful, friendly lady who gave so much back to her fans.

Few people who know of *Dracula* through the films have any real knowledge of Whitby and the town's connection with the story, and it is the intention of this book to make the connection and to show that Whitby and Dracula are inextricably linked.

There have been, regrettably, few films that have mentioned Whitby when telling the story of Dracula and this is a case of criminal neglect on the part of

The Metropole Hotel, scene of the centenary celebrations in 1997 where I met Ingrid Pitt.

My friend Richard enjoying a moment with Ingrid Pitt at the Dracula Centenary Celebrations in 1997.

Whitby's East Cliff.

the films' producers. It is Whitby where Dracula first lands in England during a violent storm, and Whitby is where he first terrorises Lucy Westenra, setting her down the path to becoming a vampire herself.

The 1979 Badham film mentions the town explicitly with most of the adventure taking place in Whitby (although Cornwall was the actual filming location). In addition to this, the previous year's BBC television adaptation of *Dracula*, featuring Louis Jordan as the Count, was actually filmed, in part, in Whitby, and for that it should be applauded. Sadly, these two productions did not receive the public exposure that they should have done and Whitby remains somewhat unknown in terms of its *Dracula* connection.

Fortunately for the visitor, Whitby remains an incredibly atmospheric town, and over 100 years later it has the added bonus that the town is virtually unchanged. The locations and views experienced by Stoker are still there today for us to experience and aid the visitor in transporting themselves back in time, into the pages of *Dracula*.

I hope that you use this book to help you relive the experiences of the novel, but beware of walking these narrow streets in the hours of darkness as you never know if that black dog watching your every move is a harmless pet or something more sinister!

Let's visit Dracula's Whitby …

Dracula: The Story

Jonathan Harker is a solicitor who journeys to Transylvania to assist Count Dracula with the purchase of a London property, namely Carfax Abbey, Purfleet. During his travels, Harker receives many warnings from the locals, begging him to stay away from Castle Dracula. Undeterred, Harker continues his journey and arrives at the castle where he meets Dracula. During his stay Harker concludes the sale of Carfax Abbey for Dracula, who insists that Harker should remain at the castle to tutor him in English customs. Many events begin to unnerve Harker and one night he is attacked by three vampire women. If not for the timely intervention of Dracula, Harker would almost certainly have been killed. However, now Harker is a prisoner within Castle Dracula.

Dracula leaves Transylvania and departs for England, taking with him fifty boxes of earth. It is Dracula's intention to spread vampirism through England. Whilst *en route* to England, Dracula takes passage aboard a Russian schooner, the *Demeter*, at Varna on the Black Sea coast. During the journey Dracula systematically kills the crew, one by one. The captain, realising that he will die, lashes himself to the ship's wheel with a crucifix in his hands. He knows that Dracula will not come near him.

During a violent storm, the *Demeter*, piloted by the dead Captain, runs aground at Tate Hill Sands in Whitby. As soon as the ship touches land a huge black dog is seen to leap from the ship and escapes into the town.

Taking their holiday in Whitby at this time are two friends, Mina Murray (Jonathan Harker's fiancée) and Lucy Westenra. Lucy is prone to sleepwalking and one night she walks to the graveyard near Whitby Abbey. Mina makes a midnight dash through the town and finds Lucy at their favourite seat in the graveyard. Lucy has suffered her first attack from Dracula.

Dracula continues to feed on Lucy until she dies, in spite of the best efforts of the Dutch doctor Abraham Van Helsing. Lucy is buried, but before long she

The First Edition cover of *Dracula* by Bram Stoker.

rises from the grave. Local children begin to talk of the 'Bloofer Lady' (a phrase that means 'Beautiful Lady') and some of them also display strange marks on their throats.

Van Helsing realises what has happened and he convinces Lucy's fiancé, Arthur Holmwood, that she is one of the undead. They open her grave and find it empty. Van Helsing and Holmwood wait and witness the vampire Lucy return to her grave. Holmwood then drives a stake through Lucy's heart, giving her eternal peace.

Meanwhile, Dracula is tormenting Renfield, a patient in the lunatic asylum run by Doctor Seward, a friend of Holmwood's. Renfield becomes obsessed with a gruesome food chain, catching flies to feed to spiders, and then feeding the spiders to birds. When Renfield's request to Seward for a cat is denied, he then eats his captive birds alive.

Harker has managed to escape from Castle Dracula and battles his way through a hostile countryside until he takes refuge at a convent. He is taken in by the nuns who nurse him back to health. Mina travels to Transylvania to be with Harker and the two of them are married before returning to England. Upon their arrival in England, Harker is shocked when he spots Count Dracula in the street, although he looks younger.

Van Helsing, Harker, Mina, Seward, Holmwood and their American friend, Quincey Morris, form an allegiance to destroy Dracula. Harker, knowing of the locations in London belonging to Dracula, leads them as they destroy Dracula's fifty boxes of soil. Leaving Mina at Seward's asylum, the vampire hunters enter Carfax Abbey and destroy the boxes there.

Mina is attacked by Dracula who flees the country, heading back to his castle in Transylvania. Van Helsing hypnotises Mina and realises that she shares a mind-link with Dracula. They are able to plot Dracula's route back to the castle.

Dracula is ambushed just outside the castle and, during a fierce battle, Harker cuts the head from Dracula and Morris plunges his knife deep into the vampire's heart, destroying him and releasing Mina from his spell.

When it was published in 1897, *Dracula* received a fair amount of praise with Stoker being described as an author of superior talent to Mary Shelley and Edgar Allan Poe. In spite of this praise, the novel was not as popular then as it is today. The success of the novel was cemented when Count Dracula made his cinematic appearances and an iconic Gothic villain was created, starting with the unauthorised 1922 film *Nosferatu*. The film was an adaptation of Stoker's story but was not officially credited to him. As a result, Stoker's widow sued the filmmaker F. W. Murnau and the resulting controversy propelled Dracula into the public consciousness, where he remains to this day.

Dracula was written as a collection of diary entries, letters, and phonograph recordings detailing the rise of the vampire threat and the subsequent quest to end Dracula's reign of terror. They are presented almost as if they are case notes for an investigation rather than as a narrative, with events often overlapping depending upon the point of view of the character in question. This technique serves to create a feeling of suspense as the reader does not know which of the characters will survive to the end of the story. It also adds a degree of realism to the story and it is this style of writing, as well as the factual basis of the story, that makes many people wonder whether *Dracula* is actually a work of fiction or a record of fact. However, it should be remembered that, when it was written, this was not a historical drama that happened many years previously, it was a contemporary horror story, something that was happening in the present day.

Dracula, although a novel based on superstition, is a story that embraces both folklore and technology, with the characters adopting scientific techniques to defeat a magical, supernatural enemy. For example, Van Helsing makes use of hypnotism (a relatively new scientific concept at the time and previously thought of as a magician's trick in the nineteenth century), blood transfusions, and, at one point, the newly invented telephone. However, in spite of his scientific knowledge, Van Helsing displays open-mindedness to areas that science cannot explain. This is demonstrated when he offers Lucy a necklace made from garlic, and seals the tombs of despatched vampires with the Host (an unleavened bread held by the Church to be the body of Jesus Christ).

In stark contrast to Van Helsing's acceptance of the supernatural, Jonathan Harker is strictly a rational thinker who dismisses the traditions and fears of the Transylvanian peasants. Even when Harker begins to experience strange events in Castle Dracula, he still looks for rational explanations until, eventually, he realises that he cannot find an explanation and suffers from what is euphemistically described as 'brain fever' as his logic cannot comprehend what is happening to him.

Much has been written academically about *Dracula*. It has been described as a book about repressed sexual feelings and the empowerment of women in Victorian society, or a metaphor for the spread of syphillis. It is, without doubt, still going to be the cause of much future discussion, but it is not the hidden themes and messages within the text that concern us at this point; rather it is the location of the main part of the story that we shall continue to explore next.

Dracula is, as we know, a work of fiction, but it had its roots in real history and real locations. Count Dracula was based upon a real person discovered by Bram Stoker in a library book in Whitby and it was in Whitby where the story was born.

The Whitby Connection

Bram Stoker was born a sickly child who remained bedridden until the age of seven due to an undisclosed illness. To entertain him his mother would tell him ghost stories and he would allow his imagination and thoughts to run riot, something that would serve him well later in life. In Stoker's youth, Gothic Horror was enjoying mass popularity due to a number of publications during the nineteenth century, but more on that later.

Stoker recovered from his childhood illnesses and became a respected civil servant, but gave it all up to manage Sir Henry Irving's Lyceum Theatre in London, a position offered to him following a favourable review Stoker wrote of Sir Henry's performance in *Hamlet*. In fact he became almost dependent upon the actor, whom he idolised in spite of the way Sir Henry treated him. Stoker remained in this post until Sir Henry's death in 1905.

In 1878 Stoker left Dublin and married the on-off sweetheart of Oscar Wilde and daughter of his neighbour at Marino Crescent, Florence Balcombe. One year later, they had a son, Noel. Now with a family, Stoker began to take holidays away from London and, in August 1890, the Stokers went to stay at Whitby on the North Yorkshire coast, staying at 6 Royal Crescent.

Also staying at 6 Royal Crescent at that time were two young sisters from Hertfordshire and their chaperone. Little did they know that they were to become the models for characters in one of the world's most popular horror stories. The sisters became Mina Murray and Lucy Westenra, and their chaperone became Mrs Westenra – Lucy's mother.

During his Whitby holiday Stoker soaked up information like a sponge. He made many notes that made their way into the text of *Dracula* in the form of observations made by Mina Murray. His favourite place to sit and plot his story was actually in the churchyard on the East Cliff overlooking the sea and the none-too-distant West Cliff and it is almost a certainty that his seat became the 'suicide's seat' where Mina and Lucy would rest. It was also to become the location where Lucy is first attacked by Dracula.

Stoker also passed the time chatting with local fishermen and the coastguard, learning of many local superstitions, myths and legends, as well as some extraordinary tales such as the wrecking of the *Dmitry*, which had occurred five years earlier. The *Dmitry* was a Russian ship from the port of Narva that dramatically ran aground during a storm on Tate Hill Sands at the foot of the East Cliff. The *Dmitry* was carrying a cargo of silver sand and Stoker would, in all probability, have heard the tale and seen pictures of this wreck during his holiday as the event was photographed by the celebrated Whitby photographer Frank Meadows Sutcliffe, famous for his sepia photographs of the town and surrounding area. Sutcliffe had just opened a gallery on the East Cliff of the town around the time of Stoker's visit. The story of this wreck obviously impressed Stoker and the wreck became part of his story as it was later renamed, by Stoker, the *Demeter* – the ill-fated ship that brings Dracula to England. In the book the ship, like its real-life inspiration, carries a cargo of silver sand and boxes of earth. The *Demeter's* home port, Varna, is an anagram of Narva.

The graveyard on the East Cliff, which was visited by Mina and Lucy.

It is Stoker's attention to detail, basing events on fact and the melding of local history, which causes so many people to wonder whether the events chronicled within the book are indeed true. It was this habit of basing the story on actual events and local legends that made it so captivating, as we shall soon see …

Perhaps the most significant date on Stoker's holiday to Whitby was 8 August 1890. This was the day that Stoker visited the Whitby Public Lending Library and read a book called *An Account of the Principalities of Wallachia and Moldavia* by William Wilkinson. Whilst reading this book Stoker found a reference to a tyrannical Eastern European prince with a penchant for impaling his enemies on large wooden stakes, as well as other acts of sadism. This man was Vlad Tepes. To his friends and enemies, he was called Dracula, meaning, the Son of the Dragon.

So excited was Stoker by his discovery that he made the date 8 August a significant date in the timeline of his story, for it became the date that the *Demeter* ran aground in Whitby harbour bringing the evil vampire to England.

Stoker also had a name for his villain now. Originally, he was to name the protagonist Count Wampyr – Wampyr meaning 'Vampire' – but now, he had a real historical character to base him upon, further increasing the credibility of his story.

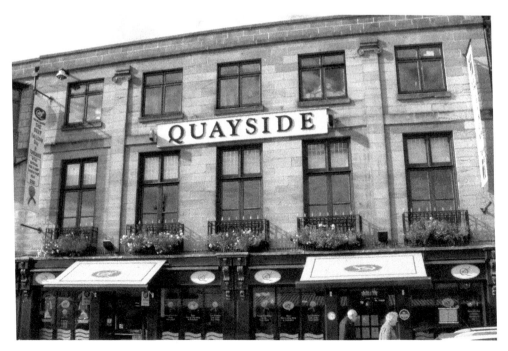

Now a fish restaurant, this building was the site of the Whitby library where Bram Stoker 'discovered' Dracula.

It is likely that Stoker wrote his Whitby sections of the book first, followed by the Carpathian chapters (as he had now 'discovered' Dracula and had changed the home of the Count from Styria to Transylvania), and finally the London portions of the book. It is interesting to note that Stoker had originally planned to set his story in Styria. As we will see later, this was also the location for the Le Fanu's classic vampire tale *Carmilla*. In keeping with his desire to make the story as believable as possible, the location was moved to the mysterious province of Transylvania and his villain named after a real person, further blurring the line between reality and fantasy.

Stoker continued to draw upon local myths and legends for inspiration, even when in London. Stoker may well have used a macabre and eerie event in London as inspiration for one of the more spine-tingling sections of his story.

Stoker had lived in Cheyne Walk, Chelsea and was a neighbour of the Pre-Raphaelite artist Dante Gabriel Rossetti (although by the time Stoker moved to Cheyne Walk, Rossetti was a recluse and the two are unlikely to have met). Rossetti's wife, Elizabeth Siddal, had died in February 1862 from an overdose of laudanum (an opium and alcohol mixture) and was buried in Highgate Cemetery. Rossetti left a small notebook of poems next to his dead wife's cheek before the coffin was sealed. Seven years later, Rossetti decided to publish the poems and had his dead wife exhumed. The exhumation took place at night by firelight and, according to legend, when the coffin was opened Elizabeth Siddal lay there as perfect as the day she had been buried. This real-life event parallels the experiences of Van Helsing and Holmwood in Lucy Westenra's tomb and it is highly likely to have inspired Stoker, firing his imagination and ultimately making its way into his story.

To keep his story as believable as possible, Stoker turned his novel into a contemporary adventure story using modern appliances and revolutionary techniques, such as typewriters, phonographs, and blood transfusions. Undoubtedly this technique won over many readers who could readily associate the events with the world in which they lived. It made the novel immensely popular and, as a result, *Dracula* was about to become a great novel and its protagonist would, ultimately, become the most famous vampire of all time.

But let us now turn our attention to the town that features so prominently in Stoker's novel...

Whitby: A History

Whitby is situated in North Yorkshire, on England's north-east coast, and is now a fishing port and tourist destination. Whitby was founded in AD 656 by the Christian King of Northumbria, Oswy. He formed the Abbey under its first abbess, Hilda (later Saint Hilda), but it was destroyed in AD 867 by Viking raiders and was not re-founded until 1078, by which time Whitby gained its name, known then as 'Hwytby' – Old Norse for 'White Settlement'.

During Hilda's tenure, Whitby became a centre of education and created the poet Caedmon who produced some of the earliest examples of Anglo-Saxon literature. Caedmon was an Anglo-Saxon who cared for the animals at Whitby Abbey. One night, while the monks were feasting, singing, and playing a harp, Caedmon left early to sleep with the animals because he did not know any songs and could not join in. In fact Caedmon was unable to put together any form of verse. While asleep, he had a dream in which 'someone' approached him and asked him to sing 'The Beginning of Created Things'. Caedmon refused to sing at first but then managed to create a short poem in praise of God.

The next morning, Caedmon remembered the song he had sung and added additional lines to his poem. He told his foreman about his dream and was taken to see the abbess who, with her counsellors, asked Caedmon about his vision. She believed that Caedmon had been gifted by God and tasked him to write a poem based on a piece of sacred history, by way of a test. When Caedmon returned the next morning with the completed poem, he was ordered to take monastic vows and was taught history and doctrine, which, after a one night, he was able to present in the form of poetry.

Today, close to St Mary's church you can find a tall cross overlooking the harbour. This is called Caedmon's Cross and was erected in memory of one of the earliest known English poets.

Whitby Abbey.

The streets of Whitby have changed little since Stoker's day and it is easy to imagine how Whitby would have been in 1890.

After the Abbey was re-founded in 1078 it was dedicated to Saint Peter and Saint Hilda but it suffered again under the reign of Henry VIII when he ordered the Dissolution. The Abbey remained empty forever after and is now the property of English Heritage and a fantastic tourist attraction.

In around 1615 several alum-producing centres sprang up around Whitby, bringing new industry to the town to serve the transportation of alum and the coal used in its production. Prior to 1615 alum was imported from the Papal States in Italy. The Papal States had the monopoly on alum production and because of its varied uses it was a valuable commodity.

Following the Dissolution, the lands that had belonged to Guisborough Priory were given to Sir Thomas Chaloner, tutor to the son of James I, Prince Henry. Sir Thomas's son, also called Thomas, travelled to the Papal States at the end of the sixteenth century to observe the alum works. Thomas Chaloner was a keen naturalist with an interest in plants and noticed that the flora and fauna around the alum works was identical to the plants that grew on his father's Guisborough estates. He realised that the rock types at the alum works were exactly the same as those back home. Realising that he could develop alum works back in England that would be independent from the Papal States, he secretly took workers from Italy and began to work alum from the rocks

Tate Hill Sands as seen from Spion Kop. In the harbour you can see the replica of the HM *Bark Endeavour* taking tourists on a trip out to sea.

near Sandsend Ness, a few miles from Whitby. Once the alum industry in England was fully established, all imports from the Papal States were banned and England became self-sufficient.

This resulted in Whitby expanding in size, wealth and yet more industry. Local oak was used in the newly formed shipbuilding industry and, as a consequence of the increased trade, import taxes allowed the town to construct twin piers, improving the harbour and further increasing trade. The shipyards at Whitby were soon to become the third largest in the country after London and Newcastle generating further wealth and industry.

The shipyards remained busy and, in 1753, the first whaling ship left Whitby, bound for Greenland; this was the beginning of the town becoming a major centre for the whaling industry. In 1814 eight whaling ships from Whitby caught 172 whales, making it the most successful year in Whitby's whaling history.

Today visitors can see the relics of Whitby's whaling industry on the West Cliff where a large archway has been constructed from the jawbones of a whale.

The Whalebone Arch on Whitby's West Cliff. At one time there were several within Whitby including one in Pannet Park where it is said that the ghost of a young boy haunted that location.

In 1839, George Hudson, the railway tycoon, successfully linked Whitby by rail with York, allowing tourists to visit the town with ease. One such tourist was none other than Bram Stoker who visited in 1890. Stoker's legacy to Whitby is seen in the thousands of visitors a year who come in search of Dracula.

Whitby also became renowned for the fossilised remains of the decayed Monkey Puzzle Tree. This product was known as jet and was found in abundance in the Whitby cliffs. Jet was mined in the Bronze Age and made into jewellery; a trend that was continued by the Romans and peaked in the mid-nineteenth century when Queen Victoria wore mourning jewellery made from jet.

Many other fossils have been found around Whitby and the best preserved are ammonite fossils, which appear on the coat of arms of Whitby town council. These fossils were known as 'snake stones' and sold in commemoration of a legend whereby Saint Hilda defeated a plague of snakes by turning them into stone. This legend became such an ingrained part of Whitby folklore that ammonite fossils were often excavated and had the heads of snakes carved into them so that they could be used as good luck charms or other such decorations. In fact, the species of ammonite, *Hildoceras*, is named after Saint Hilda. On some of the beaches can be found fossilised dinosaur footprints and the nearly complete remains of a prehistoric crocodile and a plesiosaurus have been found. Little wonder then that this stretch of coast is known as 'The Jurassic Coast'.

Whitby was also the place where Captain Cook's ship, HM *Bark Endeavour*, was built by the shipbuilder Thomas Fishburn in 1764. At the time of construction, HM *Bark Endeavour* was actually a collier named *Earl of Pembroke* and was later bought by the Royal Navy and refitted. Captain Cook was born in the town of Marton, close to Whitby, on 7 November 1728 and joined the Royal Navy in 1755 following service in the Merchant Navy as a teenager. Coincidentally, and following a dispute in the Admiralty, Cook sailed in HM *Bark Endeavour* on his first voyage of discovery to Australia and New Zealand. Cook himself was schooled as an apprentice in Whitby, staying in the home of local ship-owners and Quakers, John and Henry Walker, and his lodgings now form the Captain Cook Memorial Museum on Grape Lane.

Whitby continues to have a long association with the sea, sometimes not always for the best of reasons. There has been a lifeboat in Whitby since 1802 and it has been called out on countless occasions. In February 1861, the lifeboat sank, claiming twelve lives. Only Henry Freeman survived.

Perhaps one of the most famous rescues undertaken by the Whitby lifeboat was when it went to the aid of the hospital ship *Rohilla*, which had struck a reef at Saltwick, south of Whitby, in 1914. In total, six lifeboats were launched and the Whitby lifeboat managed to save thirty-five people in two separate attempts but was then damaged by the strong winds and tides and could no longer take part in the rescue.

The statue commemorating Captain Cook.

Today visitors can go out to sea on the *Mary Ann Hepworth*, Whitby's lifeboat from 1938 to 1974. It remains a very popular tourist attraction.

Whitby also has a more pleasant association with the sea and this takes the form of an annual regatta held for three days in August. The regatta features a rowing race where three teams – Whitby Friendship ARC, Whitby Fishermen's ARC and Scarborough ARC – compete against each other. In addition to the rowing there is a fair, military displays, fireworks, and a visit from the famous Red Arrows.

With such historical and modern-day references it is certain that Whitby will continue to attract tourists for many years to come, and it is within the world of tourism that we move in the next chapter as we investigate an area of some confusion in relation to some of the locations in *Dracula*...

What's in a Name?

As mentioned in the previous chapter, Bram Stoker lodged at 6 Royal Crescent but, before continuing, it is important to investigate a little debate that has been going on for some time. The actual location of the guest house where Stoker stayed has been attributed to approximately three locations on the West Cliff and it is this location that many cannot agree upon. It is a widely held belief that Stoker's guest house is also the guest house of Lucy Westenra and Mina Murray. So, how do we determine which premises is the correct one?

Firstly, the respected Whitby historian Colin Waters, in his book *Whitby and the Dracula Connection*, claims that the guest house where Stoker lodged was 7 Royal Crescent Avenue (now known as 7 Crescent Avenue), basing this claim on a family legend that his great-grandmother, Fanny Harker, was the landlady to Stoker. He claims that Stoker honoured the landlady by using the name 'Harker' in the novel, and that he used the address as the location for S. F. Billington, the solicitor.

The second suggestion is that Stoker stayed at 7 East Crescent as this was known as The Crescent when these nine small houses were constructed in the 1850s. It is also claimed that it was here that the heroines Lucy and Mina lodged on their fateful holiday. It is this location the Scarborough Borough Council Tourism and Leisure Service's guidebook, *Whitby Dracula Trail*, gives as the location of both Lucy and Mina's lodgings *and* the offices of S. F. Billington.

Finally, we have 6 Royal Crescent, the strongest contender to the title of Stoker's heroine's guest house, due to Stoker having been documented as lodging there.

On examination of 7 Crescent Avenue, there is very little evidence to support the claim of it being a significant address other than a story that had been passed down through several generations of Colin Water's family. It is recorded that Stoker stayed at 6 Royal Crescent as this visit was reported in the *Whitby Gazette* at the time. It states:

> *Mr, Mrs and Master Bram Stoker from London arrived in Whitby on the northeast coast of Yorkshire for their annual summer holiday, around 8th August 1890. They stayed at no.6 Royal Crescent, a house facing the sea set back from the town's West Cliff (proprietor: Mrs Veasy) in a bedroom on the third floor with a sitting room below.*

This negates Waters' claim of 7 Royal Crescent Avenue's involvement in *Dracula* on the following three points:

1. The address is clearly stated as 6 Royal Crescent.
2. The house is facing the sea. The houses on Crescent Avenue do not face the sea as the avenue runs perpendicular to the sea.
3. The proprietor is named as Mrs Veasy, not Mrs Harker (née Brown). It is not beyond the realms of possibility, and probably very likely, that Stoker may have stayed at Crescent Avenue on a different visit to Whitby but, at the time he was compiling notes for *Dracula* in 1890, and he certainly stayed at 6 Royal Crescent.

7 Royal Crescent still exists today, on the junction with John Street and Crescent Avenue; however, it is no longer a guest house but, at the time of writing, it is a delightfully named hair salon called 'Curly Tops'.

Now we move on to East Crescent, at the top of Khyber Pass. This is claimed to be the location of both Lucy and Mina's guest house and the location for the offices of Billington the solicitor in *Dracula*. This claim is made in both *The Whitby Dracula Trail* and *In Search of Dracula* by Raymond T. McNally and Radu Florescu. However, the error in the McNally and Florescu book can be directly attributed to *The Whitby Dracula Trail*, which is referenced in the Travel Guide chapter of their book. So, why is this location also incorrect? To find the answer to this we need to look at Chapter 8 of *Dracula* and the entry for 11 August where Mina writes:

> *The clock was striking one as I was in the Crescent and there was not a soul in sight. I ran along the North Terrace but could see no sign of the white figure which I expected. At the edge of the West Cliff above the pier I looked across to the East Cliff, in hope or fear – I don't know which – of seeing Lucy in our favourite seat ... I did not wait to catch another glance, but flew down the steep steps to the pier and along by the fish-market to the bridge ...*

So, Mina writes that she was in the crescent and that she ran along North Terrace to the edge of the West Cliff above the pier. To get to the cliff edge from Royal Crescent you would have to run along North Terrace. To get to the

'Curly Tops' – once a guest house and a location claimed to be where Lucy and Mina lodged in Whitby.

No. 7 East Crescent – often thought to be the guest house of Lucy and Mina. It is, in actual fact, the offices of the solicitor S. F. Billington.

The plaque indicating where Bram Stoker stayed.

same location from East Crescent you would have to run along East Terrace. This is surely strong evidence for the girl's guest house being located on Royal Crescent.

Further evidence to support this claim can be found in Mina's entry for 13 August where she describes the view from her guest house window as thus:

> *I got up and pulling aside the blind, looked out. It was brilliant moonlight and the soft effect of the light over the sea and sky – merged together in one great, silent mystery – was beautiful beyond words.*

A view of the sea would just be possible from East Terrace as the house itself faces towards the harbour and the edge of the East Cliff. But with such a fantastic view of the harbour available from this small guest house, Stoker does not make any mention of it. Although not damning evidence, when coupled with the description of the route Mina took when she left the guest house, it does suggest that 7 East Crescent is not in the right location. What we do know is that the premises is mentioned in *Dracula* and is the location of the Whitby solicitor, Mr S. F. Billington. It is therefore unlikely that the offices of a solicitor would be shared with a guest house. 7 East Crescent can still be visited today as it is a yellow-fronted guest house that takes great pride in its inclusion in *Dracula*.

So it can be seen that, on the balance of probabilities, the location of Mina and Lucy's guest house was, in fact, 6 Royal Crescent – Stoker's lodgings whilst in Whitby. Walking onto Royal Crescent, No. 6 is an unassuming, tall townhouse. It is no longer a guest house and, looking at it, it is hard to take in the literary significance of the building. All that there is to remind us is a small plaque near the front door which reads:

Whitby Civic Society
BRAM STOKER
(1847–1912)
Author of Dracula
Stayed here
1890–1896

The Whitby Chronology

Whitby first plays a significant part in *Dracula* in Chapters 6, 7, and 8. What follows is a breakdown of the events in the book relating to Whitby and the dates on which they occurred. From studying the days and dates of the week cataloguing the events in *Dracula* it shows that the story is set in 1893.

24 July

Mina Murray arrives at Whitby train station where she is met by Lucy Westenra. Together they drive up to The Crescent where their boarding house is located. Later Mina sits in the churchyard, writing in her journal about her reflections on some local legends of the Abbey and a ghostly White Lady who is seen through a window in the Abbey ruins. Mina also reflects on a legend that tells of how bells are heard out at sea when a ship has been lost. It is during this day that Mina speaks to an old sailor, Mr Swales.

26 July

Mina writes in her journal that she has not yet heard from Jonathan Harker, her fiancé, and that she is worried for him. Mina also writes of her concerns about Lucy's sleepwalking habit.

27 July

Lucy continues to sleepwalk, waking Mina as she walks around the room. Mina comments, in her journal, that it is hot and that Lucy appears rosy-cheeked.

The Bay Hotel as visited by Mina and Lucy during their visit to Robin Hood's Bay.

1 August

Mina and Lucy are in the graveyard on the top of the East Cliff when they are joined by Mr Swales. He tells them of the legends of the area and the lies that are carved on the gravestones. He illustrates this point by pointing at the tombstone laid as a slab at the feet of Lucy and Mina and explains the circumstances that led to the person buried there taking their own life.

> 'Sacred to the memory of George Canon, who died, in the hope of a glorious resurrection, on July 29, 1873, falling from the rocks at Kettleness. This tomb is erected by his sorrowing mother to her dearly beloved son. He was the only son of his mother and she was a widow.'
> 'Really Mr Swales, I don't see anything funny in that!'
> 'Ye don't see aught funny! Ha! Ha! But that's because ye don't gawm the sorrowin' mother was a hell-cat that hated him because he was acrewk'd – a regular limiter he was – an' he hated her so that he committed suicide in order that she mightn't get an insurance she put on his life.'

Later that day at 9 p.m. Mina returns to the grave. She is unhappy as she has not heard from Jonathan. Two bands play on either side of the river.

Whitby train station, where Dracula's boxes of earth were transported to London.

The band on the pier is playing a harsh waltz in good time, and farther along the quay there is a Salvation Army meeting in a back street. Neither of the bands hears each other, but up here I hear and see them both.

3 August

Mina is still worried about Jonathan and Lucy is still walking in her sleep, although to a much lesser degree. However, Mina senses that Lucy has an odd concentration about her that she cannot understand. Mina writes, 'even in her sleep she seems to be watching me.'

6 August

Mina notes in her journal that Lucy is now more excitable. Mina writes that the previous night was threatening and that fishermen say that there is a storm coming. Mina is, once again, writing her journal in the churchyard when Mr Swales approaches. Mina converses with him and Mr Swales tells her that he is feeling as if his death is near. The old sailor leaves and Mina is joined by the coastguard. The coastguard looks out to see with his spyglass and notes the presence of a strange ship far out to sea.

The guest house where Bram Stoker stayed in 1890 and where he penned much of *Dracula*. Now it is a private premises.

A view of the graveyard at St Mary's church that Mina and Lucy would visit.

Tate Hill Sands, where the *Demeter* ran aground on 8 August 1890.

A view up the Khyber Pass, built by tycoon George Hudson as a way of transporting building materials to the West Cliff.

The view from Spion Kop. The pier extensions would not have been in place in Stoker's day.

The Bram Stoker bench on Spion Kop.

The plaque on the Bram Stoker bench.

8 August

During the early hours of 8 August there is a great storm. A Russian schooner, the ship spotted by the coastguard on 6 August, is seen heading towards the harbour at high speed. When the harbour lights shine onto the ship they see the corpse of the captain, lashed to the wheel. The ship crashes on Tate Hill Sands and, at the moment of impact, a black dog is seen to bound away up the 199 steps towards the churchyard. These events are recorded in both Mina's journal and *The Daily Graph*.

9 August

The schooner is identified as being the *Demeter* from Varna and is carrying a cargo of great wooden boxes filled with mould. These are consigned to Whitby solicitor Mr S. F. Billington of 7 The Crescent, Whitby. Early in the morning the dog belonging to a local coal merchant is found dead. Its throat has been torn away and its belly slit open.

10 August

Mina records the funeral of the *Demeter*'s captain in her journal. She is saddened by the death of Mr Swales who was found in her and Lucy's seat in the churchyard. He died of a broken neck and had a look of horror on his face. During the funeral a man and his dog attend. When the dog is sat on the tombstone of the suicide near Mina and Lucy's seat it cowers in fear. Later that day Mina and Lucy walk to Robin Hood's Bay to have tea in an inn with a bay window over the seaweed-covered rocks. It is Mina's hope that this walk will stop Lucy from sleepwalking.

11 August

Mina awakes during the night in the room she shares with Lucy and realises that her friend is not there. The clock strikes one in the morning and Mina steps out onto The Crescent in search of Lucy. She runs along North Terrace to the edge of the West Cliff, just above the pier and looks across the harbour. She sees Lucy reclined in their favourite seat in the churchyard and Mina makes a mad dash through the darkened streets, across the swing bridge and up the 199 steps. At the top of the steps Mina sees something 'long and black' bending over Lucy. Mina calls to Lucy and the shape raises its head, allowing Mina to see a white face with red, gleaming eyes. When Mina reaches Lucy, the figure is gone. Lucy is having difficulty breathing and is cold. Mina wraps a shawl around her friend and leads her back to their lodgings. Mina fears that she must have pricked Lucy's neck with a large safety pin when she wrapped the shawl around her. Later that day Mina, Lucy, and Mrs

The lighthouse on the West Pier where a ghostly lighthouse keeper maintains his vigil from beyond the grave.

Whitby's harbour as it is today. Mina would have run along the harbourside to the left in her search for Lucy.

The steps leading up to the West Cliff from the Khyber Pass. Mina ran down these steps after spying Lucy in the distant churchyard.

Westenra take lunch in Mulgrave Woods and an evening stroll in Casino Terrace.

12 August

Lucy is sleepwalking again and trying to get out of the room. Fortunately Mina has locked the door, thus preventing Lucy from coming to harm.

13 August

Mina wakes in the night to find Lucy sitting up in her bed, yet still asleep. Lucy is pointing to the window and Mina goes to the glass to investigate. Outside the window is a large bat, which Mina watches as it flies towards the Abbey.

14 August

Mina and Lucy are on the East Cliff and watching the sun set. As it sets it bathes everything in a red glow. The red sunlight reflected off the windows of St Mary's church causes Lucy to utter, 'His red eyes again! They are just the same.' Later that evening Mina leaves Lucy in their room to sleep and goes for a walk along the West Cliff. On her return to The Crescent she notices, from out in the street, that Lucy is leaning out of her bedroom window. A beam of moonlight breaks the cloud and Mina sees Lucy is asleep on the windowsill and, seated next to her 'was something that looked like a good sized bird'.

17 August

Mina writes in her journal that Lucy seems to becoming weaker and that she is fading during each day. Lucy is still walking in her sleep and often sits at the open window. Mina notices the wounds on Lucy's neck and puts it down to pricking her with a safety pin when she wrapped her shawl around her a few nights previously. She also notes that the wounds do not appear to be healing. The solicitor Mr Billington has arranged for the cargo from the *Demeter* to be transferred to Carfax Abbey in London. The fifty boxes leave Whitby train station at 9.30 p.m.

18 August

Lucy and Mina sit on their favourite seat and talk. Lucy describes her dream-like memories of the night Mina found her in the churchyard.

'The Dracula Experience' on Whitby's Marine Parade – well worth a visit!

The old marketplace on Whitby's East Side. Mina would have rushed through here on her way to the 199 steps.

19 August

Mina finally receives word from her fiancé Jonathan Harker. He is in the Hospital of St Joseph and Ste Mary in Budapest. Mina leaves Whitby immediately to be with him, travelling straight to Hull to board a boat for Europe. Shortly after Mina leaves Whitby by train Lucy and her mother leave for Hillingham. Lucy and Mina never see each other again. Lucy dies on 20 September, having succumbed to Dracula's thirst for blood.

The Dracula Tour

We start our tour on 11 August 1893, following in the footsteps of Mina Murray. It is one o'clock in the morning and we can hear a nearby clock striking in the distance. If we look skyward we can see that it is overcast but, every so often, the moonlight forces itself through a gap in the clouds. Mina is looking for her friend, Lucy Westenra, who is sleepwalking and has left the guest house where they are staying.

We are on Royal Crescent (although Stoker referred to it as 'The Crescent' in his novel), outside Mina and Lucy's boarding house. It is No. 6, a tall and impressive building that doesn't look particularly sinister. But, when you realise that Bram Stoker created the world's most famous horror story from a third-floor bedroom in this house, it takes on a whole new significance. There is a Whitby Civic Society plaque on this house that tells that Bram Stoker took his holidays here.

Stoker was fond of drawing inspiration from his surroundings to use in *Dracula*, and his stay at 6 Royal Crescent was no exception. As mentioned in an earlier chapter, three ladies from Hertford were staying in the same guest house: Misses Isabel and Marjory Smith, and their chaperone Miss Stokes. They were to later to be transformed into Mina Murray, Lucy Westenra, and Lucy's mother.

As we leave, we look back to Royal Crescent. Notice that it does not seem complete. In 1827, a draper from York called George Hudson inherited a sum of £30,000 from a distant relative and set about using that money to create a rail link to Whitby and built Royal Crescent to promote tourism in the town. Hudson was so keen to see his vision completed he had the nearby Khyber Pass carved into the West Cliff to transport building materials to Royal Crescent. The pass was cut into the rock solely for this purpose. When The Crescent was only half built, Hudson ran out of money and in 1865 was imprisoned in York Castle for debt.

The swing bridge as it appears today.

However, we must rush to follow Mina as she makes her way along the edge of the West Cliff in front of Royal Crescent. She runs to the edge of the cliff above the West Pier, close to where the Captain Cook statue stands today. Below us is George Hudson's Khyber Pass, carved into the rock, which leads down to the pier. Next to us is the impressive Whalebone Arch, erected on this spot to remind people of Whitby's whaling history. Two hundred years ago, women and children would stand where we are now and watch their husbands, fathers and sons set sail for the icy North, wondering whether they would ever return.

Now, look again to your right and you can see the spur known as Spion Kop on the other side of the Khyber Pass. Spion Kop literally means 'Spy Hill', and from this point it offers some of the best views of Whitby Harbour you could hope for.

If you wish to stop a while on Spion Kop and sit and admire the view, to aid your rest you will find a bench placed in memory of Bram Stoker. The seat was a joint enterprise between Scarborough Council and the Dracula Society and was unveiled on 20 April 1980 in the presence of Bram Stoker's granddaughter, Ann Stoker. To get to the bench you will need to make your way to the top of Khyber Pass where you will see a path leading onto Spion Kop.

From this point it is possible to watch the sun rise from behind the Abbey and set behind the headland to our left. It is a strange phenomenon as the sun almost appears to be travelling from south to north – but then they do say that

The narrow streets of Whitby's East Side.

the laws of nature don't work quite the way they should when you are in the presence of a vampire!

From here we can also see St Mary's church on the East Cliff. We are with Mina again, the night has returned and the streets are dimly lit by gaslight, so faint that they can barely be seen:

There was a bright full moon, with heavy black, driving clouds, which threw the whole scene into a diorama of light and shade as they sailed across. For a moment or two I could see nothing, as the shadow of a cloud obscured St Mary's Church and all around it. Then as the cloud passed I could see the ruins of the Abbey coming into view; and as the edge of a narrow band of light as sharp as a sword-cut moved along, the church and the churchyard became gradually visible ... there on our favourite seat, the silver light struck a half-reclining figure, snowy white. The coming of the cloud was too quick for me to see much, for shadow shut down on light almost immediately; but it seemed to me as though something dark stood behind the seat ... What it was, whether man or beast, I could not tell.

St Mary's church as seen from Tate Hill Sands.

Before we move on, take a look to your left and you will see a row of nine buildings some distance away at the end of East Terrace. This is East Crescent and there now stands a guest house at No. 7. This was the location of the offices of S. F. Billington, the solicitor who took charge of Dracula's boxes of earth when they arrived in Whitby.

Mina runs down the steep steps into the dark and forbidding Khyber Pass. She has walked this route many times and can find her way with relative ease. The clouds continue to scud across the night sky, bringing brief flashes of silver moonlight to push away the shadows of the steep rocky faces on either side.

Mina presses on, her shawl wrapped tightly about her body for warmth. She reaches the deserted West Pier at the foot of this winding road. The empty pier stretches out to our left and we can see the taller of the two lighthouses, flashing its warning light at regular intervals throughout the black night. Legend has it that this lighthouse is haunted by the ghost of the unfortunate keeper who fell down the steep, slippery steps, breaking his neck. You may wish to return one stormy night to see if you can catch a glimpse of him performing his duty beyond the grave, but tonight, as Mina passes, a more mortal keeper is tending the light.

We catch up with Mina on the quayside now. To get to the East Cliff Mina must run through the Fish Quay and along Pier Road towards the swing bridge.

The foot of the 199 steps.

St Mary's church at the top of the 199 steps.

The town seemed as dead, for not a soul did I see ...

In 1890, the fish market was not the long building it is today but was composed of many stalls – boards set upon barrels, really – run by local fishermen. A long rail ran along the harbour side, next to a wide pavement with the occasional street lamp beside the rough road. In the River Esk there would be a number of fishing boats and the occasional steamer. It was a much busier place than today. The modern boats of the present day are far more advanced and, out on the street, instead of fishing folk going about their business, the sound of the amusement arcades and holidaymakers is a stark contrast. We can still follow the route that Mina took, but today it is not as open as it was in the nineteenth century, with gates and fences baring the way.

As Mina runs along the side of the River Esk she passes the Whitby Public Lending Library (now Quayside restaurant). This large building once dominated the harbourside road and was the library where Bram Stoker first discovered the real-life Dracula.

The street before it would not have been the asphalt of today but a long, sweeping street that curved along the side of the Esk. A railing runs along the riverside edge of the pavement, and spaced at regular intervals are tall gaslights.

Two graves that have been carved to show the occupations of the people buried within. The grave on the left features an easel and paint brushes, the one on the right shows a fouled anchor, indicating a person who worked at sea. Does this grave actually hold the body of the deceased or is it one of Mr Swales' 'empty graves'?

On the dark and deserted street below, under each lamp, is a pool of milky light, leading the way up the valley. Continuing past the library and following these lights Mina reaches what is now the Marine Café. She turns to the left, along the side of the harbour where the street has narrowed to only a pavement and passes 6 Marine Parade. This is the address of 'The Dracula Experience', a tourist attraction that features several waxwork scenes telling the story of Dracula. It would be unthinkable for a Dracula fan *not* to go in! If you have time, it is well worth a visit. If you don't have time, make time!

Let's continue as Mina has reached the swing bridge. There have been many bridges here in the past and in 1890 this would have been known as the 'drawbridge', a reference to an even earlier lifting bridge that was demolished in the 1830s, but the name stuck and was incorporated into Stoker's book. Even the bridge Mina crosses is not the bridge that the present-day tourist would cross. The present bridge you would use to cross now was installed in 1909 but is very similar to the one from the time of Dracula.

Let's take a moment now to look back on our route so far. Mina has run this way in a blind panic. She knows where Lucy is, far on the other side of Whitby and has run through the dark streets in her nightdress. She is running for her friend's life.

Mina is now heading for the 199 steps at the far end of Church Street; a cobbled, narrow thoroughfare that remains almost exactly as it did in Stoker's day. We are now on the east side of Whitby, with Grape Lane to our right. It is on Grape Lane, with its overhanging upper storeys, where Captain James Cook lived as an apprentice along with seventeen other young trainees. That house is now the Captain Cook museum.

Across from Grape Lane is Sandgate, which is a narrow street that runs parallel with Church Street. The shops today sell the jet jewellery that was so popular during the time of Dracula. Its popularity was boosted by Queen Victoria.

Mina runs along Church Street, its cobbled streets and irregularly spaced buildings cast deep shadows onto the street below. Today many of the public houses and inns that Mina would have run past have gone, but the dark ominous passageways and yards can still be seen, accessed through narrow gaps between the shops. They still hold an air of mystery.

As we reach the sharp right bend at the end of Church Street that will take us to the foot of the 199 steps we will see a pub called the Duke of York. Here we will make a left turn and deviate from Mina's route ever so briefly.

We now find ourselves on a small pier with a beach to our right. This is Tate Hill Sands.

The view across the harbour from the West Cliff to the churchyard. From here Mina would have seen Lucy in their favourite seat in a brief burst of moonlight.

This alleyway leads down to Tate Hill Sands where the *Demeter* ran aground during a terrible storm. It would have been up this alleyway that Dracula fled in the guise of a great black dog.

It is dark, the wind is howling and the rain lashes down with an almost unstoppable force. People on the pier clutch their hats to their heads to prevent them from being lost in the storm. The lighthouse beacon throws its light out in an urgent warning to any vessels nearby and the large coastguard lamp sweeps the harbour mouth. These are the early hours of 8 August 1893.

Without warning the tempest broke … The waves rose in growing fury … till in a very few minutes the lately glassy sea was like a roaring and devouring monster … The wind roared like thunder, and blew with such force that even strong men kept their feet, or clung with grim clasp to the iron stanchions... Masses of sea-fog came drifting inland – white, wet clouds, which swept by in ghostly fashion, so dank and damp and cold that it needed but little effort of imagination to think that the spirits of those lost at sea were touching their living brethren with the clammy hands of death …

Upon the East Cliff a searchlight shines through the storm, directing small boats to the safety of the harbour. As the light stabs into the dark heart of the storm it picks out a schooner with all sails set. Between the schooner and the harbour is a reef where many ships before have floundered and, as we watch, the ship rushes towards the reef at a great speed.

She must fetch up somewhere, if it was only in hell.

Suddenly, the schooner disappears from view in a bank of sea-fog . We can't see a thing. All we can hear is the thunder and the sea booming on and nearby rocks.

The rays of the searchlight were kept fixed on the harbour mouth across the East Pier where the shock was expected, and men waited breathless.

The destruction of the schooner upon the reef seems inevitable. We can only wait for the tragedy to unfold.

The wind suddenly shifted to the north-east, and the remnant of the sea-fog melted in the blast; and then … between the piers, leaping from wave to wave as it rushed at headlong speed, swept the strange schooner before the blast, with all sail set, and gained the safety of the harbour.

The coastguard's spotlight shines on the ship to follow her as she gains the safety of the harbour and, suddenly, the light picks out a grisly scene.

Lashed to the helm was a corpse, with drooping head, which swung horribly to and fro at each motion of the ship. No other form could be seen on deck at all. A great awe came on all as they realized that the ship, as if by a miracle, had found the harbour, unsteered save by the hand of a dead man!

The schooner hits the sands in front of us, bringing the rigging down with an almighty crash. At the precise instant the ship runs aground we see a huge black dog leap from the ship, it runs towards the East Cliff below the cemetery. It picks up speed across the sand, getting closer to the houses at the foot of the cliff. Its jaws are wide open, displaying sharp, glistening, white teeth, and then, in an instant, it is gone. Lost in the dark, uninviting alleys through which we have made our way. In the morning a coal merchant's dog will be found nearby:

> *Dead in the roadway opposite its master's yard. It had been fighting ... its throat was torn away, and its belly was slit open as if with a savage claw.*

Before we leave, the mystery of the schooner needs to be solved. It is the *Demeter* from the Russian port Varna. The captain was simply fastened to the wheel by his hands, tied using knots pulled by his own teeth. In his hands he clutches a crucifix, fixed in place by his bindings. The cords around his wrists have pulled the Captain from his seat and cut through the flesh to the bone. Whitby surgeon, J. M. Caffyn has declared the man dead for two days. In the captain's pocket is a note, sealed inside a bottle, an addition to the ship's log:

> *I dared not go below. I dared not leave the helm so here all night I stayed, and in the dimness of light I saw It – Him! God forgive me, but the mate was right to jump overboard.*

The solicitor, Mr S. F. Billington, will come and take charge of the *Demeter's* cargo – a number of wooden boxes filled with mould – and now we must continue our journey.

We retrace our path from Tate Hill Pier and must catch up with Mina as she frantically runs up the 199 steps. As we reach the Duke of York pub, to our left you will see the foot of the 199 steps.

These church steps were first mentioned in history over 600 years ago and were, until 1717, made of wood. Today the stone steps are a Grade I listed monument and recently underwent restoration, with many groups and individuals sponsoring a step.

Now, let's continue up these steps as we follow Mina.

> *The time and distance seemed endless, and my knees trembled and my breath came laboured as I toiled up the endless steps to the Abbey. I must have gone fast, and yet it seemed to me as if my feet were weighted with lead ... When I got almost to the top I could see the seat and the white figure ... There was undoubtedly something, long and black, bending over the half-reclining white figure. I called in fright, 'Lucy! Lucy!' and something raised its head, and from where I was I could see a white face and red, gleaming eyes.*

Mina rushes up the last few steps and along the path past St Mary's church. In the short time it takes to do this, she loses sight of Lucy. By the time she reaches her friend, the creature has gone. Mina fastens a shawl around her friend to keep her warm and secures it with a large safety pin before leading Lucy back through the streets of Whitby to their guest house.

When they awake in the morning she will think that she has caught Lucy's skin with the safety pin, when she sees two small wounds on her friend's neck. For the rest of their holiday, the wounds will not heal and Lucy will eventually die, a victim of Dracula.

Lucy and Mina have left us now, heading back down the 199 steps and then to their boarding house. Sadly, we can no longer visit their favourite seat. Many of the graves have disappeared as the cliff has subsided during the passage of time. Stay awhile on this cliff-top retreat, but beware, Dracula may still be haunting this very place.

In Search of Dracula's Grave

The last chapter left us in St Mary's churchyard at the top of the 199 steps and it is definitely worth taking a little while to examine this curious location. In Stoker's day the churchyard was much bigger than it is now; erosion and landslides have taken their toll and many graves have been lost. However, some memorials remain and you can still see some of the gravestones remembering the victims of the 1861 Lifeboat Disaster propped against the church.

Just above is the ancient sundial with its eerie inscription: 'Our Days Pass Like A Shadow'. If nothing else, this message only adds to the atmosphere of the place and leaves the visitor feeling that they are, indeed, in a very mysterious place.

Many visitors to Whitby will climb the steps to visit this graveyard with the sole intention of finding Dracula's grave, and this chapter will guide you through a collection of the more curious memorials that can be found here. We shall look at some of the many contenders for Dracula's grave, as well as discovering the last resting places of famous literary figures such as Humpty Dumpty and Tom Thumb.

When we follow the path towards the Abbey we will find the first, most promising candidate for Dracula's grave, close to the churchyard exit. To the side of the path you will notice two very low graves with no writing on them yet, when you examine the ends, you will clearly see a skull and crossbones carved into the sandstone. These gruesome stones must surely be the final resting place of a supernatural creature! Alas not. These two graves are all that remains of three tabletop graves known locally as 'The Pirates' Graves'.

However, in spite of the romantic name, these are not even the final resting places of pirates, but more likely the graves of Master Freemasons.

Thought by many to be benches, these are actually coffin rests on the 199 steps.

It is believed that Freemasons of the Third Degree, otherwise known as Master Masons, often used the skull and crossbones on their resting places to symbolise the Skull of Sidon – a tale of great significance in Freemasonry and Templar legend. The skull and crossbones became a great symbol of protection after the strange events of the Templar Lord of Sidon. Forbidden to love, he had a relationship with a lady named Maraclea who died suddenly. Months after her burial he returned to the grave and exhumed her body on the instruction of a strange, disembodied voice. Within the grave he found the skull resting on the crossed leg bones. The same disembodied voice told him that the bones would become the provider of great things and would protect him. Indeed, the Lord of Sidon needed only to show the skull to his enemies and they were defeated. After his death, the skull fell into the hands of the Templars.

The next most likely candidate can be found a short distance away from the Pirates' Graves. It is a grave made entirely of iron.

In order to protect yourself from a vampire, it is believed that either the cross or crucifix was the best weapon. However, before religious symbols were readily employed in this method there were many folk remedies used. Garlic was the most popular and well-known vampire repellent, as well as hawthorn and rowan woods. Another defence was scattering seeds, as the vampires were supposed to become so involved in counting every single seed, one by one, that they would either lose interest, or be caught counting even as the sun came up.

The enigmatic inscription on the sundial on the side of St Mary's church.

Surprisingly, silver was not as traditional a protective metal as supposed in popular fiction – iron was the metal of choice. Iron shavings were placed beneath a child's cradle, a necklace with an iron nail could be worn, and other iron objects were placed strategically around the home to ensure vampires were kept well at bay. So surely a grave made of iron will keep Dracula from rising? This must be Dracula's grave!

In fact it is the grave of the engineer George Chapman and is one of only a few metal grave markers in the country. I have only ever seen one other metal grave marker, in the parish church at Gisburn on the Lancashire/Yorkshire border.

The grave at Whitby was commissioned before Chapman's death and cast at Baxtergate foundry. It has, sadly, fallen into some disrepair and the iron urn that once topped this impressive memorial is no longer present. So we must continue our search for Dracula's grave. Whilst we look, there are a few interesting facts about the graveyard to share. To reach the cemetery it is very likely that you would have used the 199 steps. At intervals there are a number of benches set on large flat areas. These benches are truly a wonderful place to sit and watch the harbour or admire the red roofs of Whitby, but they were never designed to provide a place of rest for tourists. Instead they were constructed to act as 'coffin rests' for weary pall-bearers as they carried the coffins to the graveyard.

The Engineer's Grave – a rare example of a cast-iron grave.

The gravestone listing the victims of the 1861 Lifeboat Disaster.

Another cast-iron grave marker found in a churchyard in Gisburn.

William Scoresby's grave.

The skull and crossbones is visible at the end of one of the Pirate's Graves.

The graveyard is also the last resting place of the Arctic explorer William Scoresby, the inventor of the crow's nest used on ships as a lookout point. And, as would be expected of a maritime town, many graves mark the resting places of those who lost their lives at sea. But this graveyard continues to provide little quirks that add to the mystery of the place. For example, local tales speak of a grave that bore the contradictory inscription, 'Here lies the body of Isaac Green whose body was lost at sea and never found'.

Mina and Lucy's old friend, Mr Swales, made mention of these 'empty' graves when talking to the pair on one of their many walks:

> *'Look here all around you in what airt you will. All them steans, holdin' up their heads as well as they can out of their pride, is acant, simply tumblin' down with the weight o' the lies wrote on them, "Here lies the body" or "Sacred to the memory" wrote on all of them, an' yet in nigh half of them bean't no bodies at all...'*

As mentioned before, the graves of childhood heroes Humpty Dumpty and Tom Thumb can also be found within the graveyard, close to each other.

Between two graves is a tiny headstone, believed by many Whitby children to be Tom Thumb's last resting place. In reality it is probably the grave of an infant between his two parents. Sadly the inscriptions are worn away and can no longer be fully read, but you may be able to make out the letters *I* and *W* carved on the tiny headstone. The headstone to the left marks the grave of Isaac Woodhouse. Is the smaller grave that of his son or daughter?

A large oval gravestone close by has also been claimed to hold the shattered pieces of the nursery rhyme character, Humpty Dumpty. The sandstone has been weathered to the point where nothing more can be read on the grave. You may argue then that it could possibly be the grave of Humpty Dumpty. However, the nursery rhyme character was never an anthropomorphic egg but rather a famous cannon that was perched atop a great defensive wall. In battle it was dislodged and came crashing down, the cast metal shattering on impact and destroying the weapon permanently.

We are still no closer to finding Dracula's grave in St Mary's graveyard, and many a knowing local will tell you with authority that Dracula was never buried in this graveyard. This is true, Dracula was never *buried* in this graveyard, but that doesn't mean that he never stayed in this graveyard. Stand now in front of St Mary's church and look over the harbour. When the *Demeter* crashed on Tate Hill Sands it contained fifty boxes of earth, which were swiftly taken into the care of Samuel Billington, the solicitor. These were transported by Dracula for him to use as places to rest. A vampire can only rest in their own soil or in the grave of a suicide. At our feet would have been the gravestone of just such a suicide. The inscription would be all but worn away and unreadable but it was in this grave where Dracula rested whilst in Whitby. Tread carefully now!

The tiny gravestone is supposed to mark the last resting place of Tom Thumb.

This oval-shaped grave is believed to hold the pieces of Humpty Dumpty.

The monument to William Scoresby – inventor of the Crow's Nest – near to Whitby train station.

Whitby's Ghosts and Legends

As we spent the last chapter looking at some of the famous graves of Whitby's cemetery, and discovered some of the intriguing myths surrounding those graves, I feel that it is only fitting that we should now take the time to look at a few of the other legends that have created the shroud of mystery that would have certainly have inspired Bram Stoker when writing his book. We have already experienced one of these legends as we passed the lighthouse when we followed Mina through the streets, but there are many more stories to be told.

As we have seen earlier, Stoker spoke extensively to locals and listened to their tales, weaving them into his own work, but it would have been impossible for him to have included every single ghost story that Whitby has to offer. Indeed it would probably take another book to catalogue each of the legends, so I have taken the liberty of choosing a few of the better-known stories that surround this quiet fishing town...

The first tale features the spectral hound known as the Barguest, a Yorkshire word meaning 'town ghost'. There are many tales of Barguests amongst Yorkshire and beyond, and it is believed that this fearsome spectre often takes the form of a monstrous black dog with sharp teeth and claws.

Sir Arthur Conan Doyle, the creator of Sherlock Holmes, was inspired by tales of a phantom black dog in Norfolk that led to his famous tale *The Hound of the Baskervilles*. But he was by no means the first author to have been inspired by Black Dog legends. By now you will have made the link between the Barguest of Whitby and the mysterious black dog that leapt from the stricken ship *Demeter* as it ran aground on Tate Hill Sands.

Whitby's own Black Dog would prowl the streets of Whitby and the nearby moors after dark. Any person who heard the unholy howl of the Barguest would be sure to die before the morning arrived. Was the Barguest a real being?

Or was it simply a means of frightening people into staying inside at night, safe behind a locked door?

Another mention of the Barguest in Whitby features something different to a large Black Dog. If you recall, the word Barguest means 'town ghost' and can therefore apply to any sort of ghost. Our next legend features a ghostly coach and horses that would visit the town.

It is rumoured within Whitby that a sailor from the town who perished would be visited in his grave a few days later. On the third night after their funeral a ghostly coach pulled by a number of headless horses would thunder towards the cemetery at St Mary's church. On board the coach would be a group of skeletal sailors come to pay their respects to their colleague. The coach would then make three laps of the grave, which would cause the ghost to leave the grave and join the other spectres before disappearing into the night.

Smugglers, however, were well known for using ghost stories to cover up their activities to keep witnesses away from their activities. The coffin of a sailor would make an excellent place to hide smuggled goods and could easily be recovered so soon after the funeral. There are accounts of smugglers in Dorset actually painting their horses white, except for the heads, and hanging lanterns about the coach to give the impression of glowing phantom carriage. Could that same tactic have been employed in Whitby?

Talk of smuggling leads us quite nicely to the Old Smuggler Café on Baxtergate. The Old Smuggler is believed to date as far back as 1401 and was once called The Old Ship Launch Inn. The Old Smuggler had a long involvement in smuggling and stands on the site of a smuggling tunnel that leads to a nearby pub – the Station Inn.

Just outside of the Old Smuggler is a carved wooden figure, the origins of which are long forgotten, but a popular story tells us that it is part of a captured French smuggling vessel. With such a rich history it seems only right that this former inn should have its own ghost and indeed it does. However, whatever it is that haunts the atmospheric café, it does not appear in any visual form. It is more of an invisible force that has been reported to push gently at people inside the building as if making its presence known.

Not far from the Old Smuggler is Pannet Park. The park is home to the town's museum and features, amongst its exhibits, a gruesome device to assist in Whitby's criminal fraternity. The 'Hand of Glory' is a severed hand cut from the arm of a convicted criminal whilst the body still hung from the gibbet. When used correctly, it would act as a torch as well as magically preventing the occupants of a house from waking when it was being burgled.

According to legend, to prepare a Hand of Glory, first it would have to be drained of all blood and then embalmed in a mixture of saltpetre, salt and pepper for fourteen days before being dried out in the sun. That would prepare the hand but it still required a magical candle that would need to be made from the fat from the corpse of a hanged man, wax, and sesame from Lapland. This candle would be placed between the fingers of the mummified hand and lit when the burglary was about to take place.

Also in the museum you will find a 'witch post' from East End Cottage, Egton. Witch posts are almost exclusively a feature of the area around Whitby and the North York Moors. A witch post is a solid, upright timber of rowan wood which is built as part of a house's structure, often by the fireplace. It has a carved cross near the top of the post and it is believed that their purpose was to protect the house and its inhabitants from witches, as Rowan was thought to have magical, protective properties; so much so that it was also known as 'Witchwood'. It is also possible that priests in the earlier times who stayed in the house may have blessed the house and its occupants, and the occasion was marked by the carving of a cross on one of these posts.

Whilst we are visiting Pannet Park it is worth mentioning a tale recounted by Colin Waters in his book *Gothic Whitby*. Colin tells the tale of a young boy who appeared in a distressed state near to an ancient whalebone arch. It has been speculated that this boy may have been one of many cabin boys who left on the whaling ships and never returned. These poor souls may have drowned, frozen to death in the ships' rigging or, more sinisterly, have been killed as whaling ships would have been trapped in the Arctic ice for weeks on end. When food supplies ran short dogs, rats, and possibly even the cabin boys, would have been used as a means of preventing starvation. It is said that when the whalebone arch in Pannet Park was removed the ghost of the young boy disappeared.

Just outside of Pannet Park is the famous Bagdale Hall, built in the early 1500s as a manor house for James Conyers – bailiff to the abbot of Whitby Abbey. It is in this hall where the Royalist officer, Browne Bushel, once stayed prior to his execution for treason in 1651 after he swapped sides on the Roundheads during the English Civil War in 1643. It is believed that his headless ghost still roams the hall's uppermost floors.

There must have been something about Bagdale Hall as in 1631 it already had a reputation as a place where odd things took place. It changed hands many times over the years with many an odd tale in tow. In the late 1800s the building was quickly becoming derelict and was soon shut completely. It became a place to be avoided by locals who claimed to have seen mysterious lights from within.

Bagdale Hall was due to be sold again in the 1900s and its reputation as a haunted house was much debated. This argument, between local councillors, culminated in a bet taken by a sceptical politician to spend a night in the hall. Legend has it that he lasted until just after midnight when the building had 'unexplainably come alive'. Today it is a hotel so you can, if you dare, stay the night yourself. I am told that a very comfortable night can be had at Bagdale Hall these days.

In *Dracula*, Mina Harker makes reference to a ghost of a white lady in the ruins of Whitby Abbey, so let's examine this particular legend more closely...

It is a most noble ruin, of immense size, and full of beautiful and romantic bits; there is a legend that a white lady is seen in one of the windows.

Mina Murray's Journal
24 July

Such was the legend of the white lady, believed to be the ghost of Saint Hilda herself, that people from miles around would visit Whitby Abbey between ten and eleven o'clock in the morning. Sure enough, on a bright day they would be blessed with the sight of Saint Hilda walking past the uppermost windows on the Abbey's north side wrapped in a white shroud. Sadly, this was nothing more than a convincing optical illusion caused by the sun on the window but it was enough to create the foundations of a legend that lasted many, many years.

Just beneath the East Cliff, on Church Street is a wonderful establishment called the White Horse and Griffin. It operates as a hotel and restaurant and is well worth a visit. The White Horse and Griffin is also home to some alleged haunting, and there were rumours that a reward was offered to any person who could spend a night alone in that place.

In the 1980s the White Horse and Griffin was a museum of oddities from the Victorian era and beyond. I heard a tale that in the late 1980s a visitor to Whitby and his girlfriend visited this museum. The exhibits were displayed on many different floors of the building and one of the exhibits was a display of the character of Mrs Havisham from *Great Expectations* and the Ghosts of Christmas from *A Christmas Carol*. The young man and his girlfriend did not initially find anything particularly eerie about the exhibition, but then, and without explanation, something seized their senses and they both fled the room in fear. They returned to the room a few moments later, having composed themselves, but still the room had a strange feeling of dread about it and the pair left the room, and the museum, shortly afterwards. Today, visitors to the White Horse and Griffin can stay in a room called the Dickens room. Is this the same room where the strange occurrence took place?

Staying with the White Horse and Griffin briefly, the tale of strange goings on continues. Sometime after the museum closed and before it became a hotel and restaurant, a skeptical local man decided to see if there was any truth in the stories of ghostly goings on in the building. He broke into the empty building, taking with him a tape recorder to document his stay. According to the tale, he fled the building a few hours later, thereafter a firm believer in ghosts! His tape recorder had, allegedly, picked up the sounds of footsteps both walking and running, the noise of doors slamming, and a sound that he described as the cracking of a whip.

Not far from the White Horse and Griffin was a pub called the Turk's Head, which has long since been demolished. It was located at 73 Church Street and, although it did not technically have a ghost, it was the scene of a very strange event. The pub itself was not a very attractive place and was subject to unsavoury rumours that suggested that the landlord was in league with the Devil. This landlord must have been a particularly sinister and frightening man and his reputation was no doubt enhanced when, one day, he vanished from the pub, taking one of the barmaids with him. The departure was so sudden and inexplicable that locals could only draw one conclusion, that the pair had run off with one another. Nothing was ever seen or heard of the landlord again but the same could not be said about the barmaid. Local legend tells that when the Turk's Head was undergoing some renovation work a box was discovered that contained the skeleton of a woman. Was this the missing barmaid, murdered by the landlord who fled to avoid prosecution?

Not far from the site of the Turk's Head is Grape Lane, where Captain Cook once lodged when he was an apprentice. Grape Lane was once home to the Whitby Archives, and it has been reported that the ghost of an old sailor has been seen walking along a corridor in the cellar. Could this be the ghost of some poor unfortunate, lost at sea, who returns to his favourite lodgings?

I have recounted only a very small number of ghost stories and legends that occur in Whitby, there are many more intriguing tales to discover and the best way to do that would be to take one of the many ghost walks of Whitby that run most nights from various locations within the town. I have enjoyed these evening walks many times, listening to the guide's exciting and interesting tales whilst being wrapped in a light sea mist that only adds to the eerie atmosphere that makes Dracula's Whitby so powerful!

Dracula and the Goths

A Gothic festival that originally began as an *ad hoc* gathering of forty friends back in 1994 is held in Whitby twice a year. It is called 'Whitby Gothic Weekend' and is often abbreviated to WGW. It started as an annual gathering until the centenary of the publication of *Dracula* in 1997; WGW then became a twice-yearly event. It is attended by people who dress in period clothing or punk outfits, often in black. They listen to a particular type of music and follow a particular culture. These people are the Goths and you cannot visit Whitby without seeing or hearing about them.

But what is a Goth? The original Goths were an East Germanic tribe instrumental in the fall of the Roman Empire. As a result, the Romans regarded the Goths as uncultured and barbaric.

Later, during the Renaissance period, medieval architecture began to be regarded as unfashionable, barbaric, and lacking the culture of modern styles and was given the label 'Gothic'. Ideas soon changed and, during the 1700s in Britain, a nostalgia for all things medieval led to a fascination for Gothic ruins and, ultimately, romance, religion and the supernatural. Followers of Gothic revival were nicknamed 'Goths' and the first use of this term to describe those of a particular culture appeared in modern language.

Horace Walpole is credited with founding the Gothic novel in 1764 with the publication of the 'real' medieval romance, *The Castle of Otranto*, which he claimed to have discovered and republished. In creating this back story he created the Gothic novel's association with fake documentation to increase the validity of the story. This is used to great effect in *Dracula* where the book is seemingly composed of letters and journal entries. The term Gothic was now associated with a mood of morbidity, melodrama, horror and the supernatural. This genre was soon to include an enchanting element – the Gothic Villain – the most famous example being, of course, Count Dracula.

The bench erected to the memory of Sophie Lancaster.

The Gothic Villain was essentially a European aristocrat who dwelt in a ruinous castle or lavish stately home. He – and generally they were male – would have some dastardly plot or attempt to destroy the moral fabric of society.

The Goth culture of today, especially within the United Kingdom, started life during the late 1970s and early 1980s in the Punk offshoot known as Gothic Rock. The Gothic Rock movement became a recognisable entity in terms of fashion and a macabre, esoteric music and outlook. The bands that formed the early Gothic Rock movement included Bauhaus, Siouxsie and the Banshees, The Damned, and The Cure. These were bolstered in the mid-1980s by other groups, such as Sisters of Mercy, The Mission, and Fields of the Nephilim.

In the mid-1990s, the music had evolved further as it began to incorporate other alternative music styles. The variety of styles came about as a need to attract a wide audience at music venues, as well as an attempt to appeal to a wider market but, at its heart, the Goth movement still followed supernatural and occult themes.

As the Goth culture flourished it became more and more synonymous with horror novels and films. When Anne Rice began to write about her vampire characters, they were often lonely and melancholic, thus making them attractive to Goths of the '80s and '90s who came to adopt this outlook. When Rice's stories were later filmed they depicted Goths as characters and provided an inspiration for fashion within the subculture.

Gothic inspiration was also drawn from figures from the nineteenth century such as Lord Byron or fictional characters with similar attributes of moodiness, arrogance, and mystery. Dracula was, of course, typical of this and was quickly embraced and assimilated into the Goth subculture, partly due to the portrayal of Dracula made famous by Bela Lugosi.

In fact, Lugosi was the inspiration for the 1979 song 'Bela Lugosi's Dead' by the band Bauhaus. The song is thought to be the first Goth rock song produced and featured in the opening sequence of the 1983 vampire film *The Hunger*.

The early Goths were similar in appearance to punks except that their clothing was black. Goth fashion is often stereotyped as being dark and morbid

The appeal of Whitby to Goths has led to specialist shops being established within the town.

and featuring dark make-up and dyed black hair. However, the clothing worn has since diversified from its punk origins and now often features black period-style clothing from the Victorian or Edwardian eras.

In spite of this, Goth fashion is frequently confused with Heavy Metal fashion, which leads to the Goth culture being regarded with some suspicion due to the actions of people having no involvement with Goths. The Gothic fascination with the supernatural has led the world's media to paint an unfair image of the Goth as an outsider capable of undermining the fabric of society. A number of killings in American schools, such as the Columbine High School massacre, sadly increased this moral panic by wrongly associating those responsible with the Goth culture when, in fact, they were fans of Heavy Metal music. As a result of this public confusion, many Goths often experience prejudice and intolerance because of their membership of this movement.

On 11 August 2007, Sophie Lancaster and her boyfriend Robert Maltby were brutally attacked whilst walking through a park in Bacup, Rossendale. They both suffered serious head injuries. Tragically, Sophie never recovered and she died from her injuries. The attack was believed to be provoked simply by the fact that Sophie and Robert were Goths. Following Sophie's death her mother, Sylvia Lancaster, helped set up a fund called S.O.P.H.I.E – meaning Stamp Out Prejudice, Hatred and Intolerance Everywhere.

In January 2008, a memorial bench was erected on Whitby's West Cliff in memory of Sophie.

Goths, by the nature of their culture, are non-violent, passive and apolitical, and being a Goth can often be seen as being a valuable experience for the individual both culturally and in creative terms. When you look at other subcultures that formed in the eighties, such as the New Romantics, they have all but died out but the Goth culture continues to survive as if it were immortal, which is quite apt given the subject of their inspiration.

So why do Goths come to Whitby? It is believed by some that Whitby was chosen as a result of its connections with *Dracula* and its compatibility with the Goth movement, yet other sources claim that it was due to the locals' acceptance of the vampire legend within the town that made it more tolerant towards a group of people with their own particular style of music and fashion. Whichever is true, Whitby, Goths and *Dracula* are inseparable and are likely to continue their unique relationship for a very long time to come, especially with the Whitby Goth Weekend being run twice a year. This event is considered to be the definitive Goth event in the United Kingdom, attended by Goths from all over the country.

The Whitby Gothic Weekends are big business for tourist industries in Whitby, and during the events most hotels and guest houses are totally booked up. Goth bands can be found playing in many of the town's pubs, and many other events take place such as markets and charity fundraising events. In 2007, the WGW raised money to erect the Sophie Lancaster bench on the West Cliff.

The Whitby Gothic Weekend website modestly states that the biannual event is one of the world's premier Goth events. The continued success and fame of these events shows that the interest in all things Gothic and Whitby's Dracula connections show no sign of dying off.

The Real Dracula

Vlad Tepes, the man who became known as Dracula, was born in November or December 1431, in the fortress of Sighisoara, Romania. His father, Vlad Dracul, was, at that time, the appointed military governor of Transylvania. He had been inducted into a group known as the Order of the Dragon about one year before. The order was both a military and religious society, originally created in 1387. The aims of the order of knights were to protect the interests of Catholicism, and to crusade against the Turks.

'Dracul' in the Romanian language means 'Dragon', and the boyars of Romania, who knew of Vlad Tepes's father's induction into the Order of the Dragon, decided to call him 'Dracula'. Dracula means 'the Son of the Dragon' and was the surname to be used ultimately by Vlad Tepes.

In the winter of 1436/37, Dracul became Prince of Wallachia (one of the three Romanian provinces) and took up residence at the palace of Tirgoviste, the princely capital. Vlad Tepes followed his father and lived six years at the princely court. In 1442, for political reasons, Dracula and his younger brother Radu were taken hostage by the Turkish Sultan Murad II. Dracula was held in Turkey until 1448, while his brother Radu decided to stay there until 1462. The Turks set him free after informing him of his father's assassination in 1447 – organised by Vladislav II. He also learned about his older brother Mircea's death. Mircea was the eldest legitimate son of Dracul and he had been tortured and buried alive by the boyars of Tirgoviste.

At seventeen years old, Vlad Dracula, supported by a force of Turkish cavalry and a contingent of troops, made his first major move toward seizing the Wallachian throne. But another claimant, none other than Vladislav II himself, defeated him only two months later. In order to secure his second and major reign over Wallachia, Dracula had to wait until July of 1456, when he had the satisfaction of killing his mortal enemy and his father's assassin.

A portrait of Vlad Tepes.

Die facht sich an gar ein grauffen

liche erschiockenliche hyftoiien von dem wilden reütnch.
Dracole wayde. Wie er die leüt gespift hat. vnd gepiaten.
vnd mit den haüßtern yn einem keffel gefoten. vñ wie er die
leüt gefchunden hat vñ zerhacken laffen als ein kraut. Jtez
er hat auch den müternn ire kind gepiate vnd fy habes müf-
fen felber effen. Vnd vilandere erschiockenliche ding die in
diffem Tractat geschiiben ftend. Vnd in welchem land er
geregiret hat.

An early woodcut featuring Dracula feasting within a forest of impaled victims.

Vlad then began his six-year reign, during which he committed many cruel acts, and hence established his fearsome reputation.

His first major act of revenge was aimed at the boyars of Tirgoviste for the killing of his father and his brother. On Easter Sunday, 1459, he arrested all the boyar families who had been responsible. He impaled the older ones on stakes and forced the others to march from the capital to the town of Poenari. This fifty-mile trek was gruelling, and those who survived were not permitted to rest until they reached destination. Dracula then ordered them to build him a fortress on the ruins of an old outpost overlooking the Arges River. Many died in the process. Dracula succeeded in creating a new nobility and obtaining a fortress for future emergencies. Today the remains of the building are identified as Castle Dracula.

Dracula became famous for his brutal punishment techniques; he often ordered people to be tortured and killed in the most painful ways possible.

In 1459, Dracula was visited by Turkish envoys to collect taxes for the Sultan. Dracula realised that to pay such taxes would made a public acceptance that Wallachia was part of the Ottoman Empire. The envoys were presented to Dracula but did not remove their headdress in Dracula's presence. Enraged, Dracula asked them why they did not show him the correct respect and remove their headdress. The envoys are reported to have replied that it was their custom to not remove their headdress. Dracula responded that he should like them to strengthen their customs and ordered that the envoys be held until his men obtained some long nails, which Dracula used to secure the envoys' headdresses to their skulls. However, his most infamous and favourite method was impalement on stakes, hence the surname Tepes, which means 'the Impaler' in the Romanian language.

There are many anecdotes about the philosophy of Vlad Dracula. He was known throughout his land for his fierce insistence on honesty and order. Almost any crime, from lying and stealing to killing, could be punished by impalement. Being so confident in the effectiveness of his law, Dracula placed a golden cup on display in the central square of Tirgoviste. The cup could be used by thirsty travellers, but had to remain in the square. According to the available historic sources, it was never stolen and remained entirely unmolested throughout Dracula's reign.

As strange as it may seem, Dracula was a man who believed in right and wrong and this was demonstrated when a merchant from Florence visited Tirgoviste. The merchant travelled with a great deal of money and asked Dracula to provide soldiers to act as security for his wealth. He was told to leave the money in the public square and offered lodgings in Dracula's palace, assured that his money was safe.

Unfortunately, during the night, a thief helped himself to 160 golden ducats from the merchant's fortune. The merchant discovered his loss and reported it to Dracula who promised that the money would be returned and the thief apprehended. In total secrecy Dracula replaced the gold ducats from his own treasury and added one more ducat, bringing the total to 161.

Dracula then ordered the residents of Tirgoviste to seek out the thief or he would destroy their homes.

The merchant was allowed to check his money and realised that all his money had been returned, with the addition of an extra ducat. He reported back to Dracula telling him that his money had returned and that there was an extra ducat included. At that moment the thief was brought before Dracula and the merchant and impaled. Dracula told the merchant that had he not admitted to having found the extra ducat then he would have been impaled along with the thief.

Another tale tells the story of Dracula's love of honesty, and his own vanity. Benedict de Boithor was a Polish nobleman in the service of the King of Hungary who visited Dracula at Tirgoviste in September of 1458. At dinner one evening Dracula ordered that a golden spear be brought and set up directly in front of the royal envoy. Dracula then asked the envoy why he thought this spear had been set up. Benedict replied that he imagined that some boyar had offended the prince and that Dracula intended to honour him. Dracula then responded that he had, in fact, had the spear set up in the honour of his noble

Mehmed II – the Turkish Sultan who Vlad the Impaler waged war against.

Polish guest. The Pole then responded that had he done anything to deserve death then Dracula should do as he thought best. He further asserted that in that case Dracula would not be responsible for his death; rather he would be responsible for his own death for incurring the displeasure of the prince. Dracula was greatly pleased by this answer and showered the man with gifts while declaring that had he answered in any other manner he would have been immediately impaled.

Dracula was also very concerned that all his subjects work and be productive to the community. He looked upon the poor, vagrants and beggars as thieves. On one occasion he invited all the poor and sick people of his kingdom to his court in Tirgoviste for a great feast. After the guests ate and drank, Dracula spoke to them and asked them if they had dined well. The guests replied that they had and Dracula then asked them if they wished to be free from poverty and hardship. The guests answered that they would and at that moment Dracula ordered the hall boarded up and set on fire. No one survived.

Dracula was also keen to ensure that people worked hard in his land. Tales tell that he once noticed a man working in the fields who was wearing a caftan that was shabby and short by several sizes. Dracula stopped and asked the man whether or not he had a wife. When the man answered that he did, Dracula had the woman brought before him and asked her how she spent her days. The poor, frightened woman stated that she spent her days washing, baking and sewing. Dracula pointed out her husband's short caftan as evidence of her laziness and dishonesty and ordered that she be impaled, despite her husband's protestations that he was well satisfied with his wife. Dracula then ordered another woman to marry the peasant but admonished her to work hard or she would suffer her predecessor's fate.

In the beginning of 1462, Dracula launched a campaign against the Turks along the Danube River. It was quite risky as the military force of Sultan Mehmed II was far more powerful than Dracula's army. However, during the winter of 1462, Dracula was very successful and gained many victories.

To punish Dracula, the Sultan decided to launch a full-scale invasion of Wallachia and, with an army three times larger than Dracula's, it was the Sultan's intention to transform the land into a Turkish province.

Finding himself without allies, Dracula was forced to retreat towards Tirgoviste. He burned his own villages and poisoned the wells so that the Turkish army would find nothing to eat or drink.

When the Sultan finally reached the capital city, he was confronted by a gruesome sight: thousands of stakes held the remaining carcasses of some 20,000 Turkish captives, a horror scene that was ultimately nicknamed the 'Forest of the Impaled'. This terror tactic by Dracula was definitely successful; the scene had a strong effect on the Sultan's forces and they admitted defeat. Sultan Mehmed retreated and left the next phase of the battle to Dracula's younger brother Radu, the Turkish favorite for the Wallachian throne. At the head of a Turkish army and joined by Dracula's detractors, Radu pursued his brother to Poenari castle on the Arges River.

During this pursuit a messenger fired an arrow into Poenari Castle, warning of the approach of Radu's army. The letter was read by Dracula's wife who, preferring death to capture by the Turks, threw herself from the castle tower into the Arges River below. This event was referenced in the film Bram Stoker's Dracula but, in the film, it was highly romanticised and was used as the catalyst for Dracula's turn from Christianity.

Dracula managed to escape the siege of his fortress by using a secret passage into the mountain. Helped by some peasants of a nearby village, he was able to reach Transylvania where he met the new King of Hungary, Matthias Corvinus, seeking help. However, instead of providing some help, Matthias arrested Dracula and imprisoned him at the Hungarian capital of Visegrad. It was not until 1475 that Dracula was again recognised as the Prince of Wallachia. It was a very short reign as he was assassinated toward the end of December 1476.

An account of Dracula's death stated that his army began to kill the Turks and, in order to get a better view, Dracula climbed a nearby hill. Whether or not he was mistaken for a Turk, killed by Turks, or whether some of his own men turned against him, we will never know, but the account states that Dracula was struck with a lance. Dracula fought back, killing several of his own men, but was again struck many times and ultimately died.

The identity of the assassin was never known but Dracula's death undoubtedly happened in the midst of battle. Following his death, Dracula was decapitated and his head transported to Constantinople where it was displayed as proof that Dracula was indeed dead.

But there was still a further mystery to be uncovered. Dracula's headless body was buried at Snagov chapel on a remote Lakeland island. In 1931 genealogist, George Florescu and archaeologist Dinu Rosetti excavated Snagov. When they excavated Dracula's grave they did not find the headless skeleton of the prince but a deep hole filled with animal bones.

In actual fact, Dracula was not buried at Snagov; this had been a fictional tradition established in the nineteenth century. After Dracula's death his head was taken to Constantinople, as mentioned earlier, but his body was buried at Comana Monastery – a monastery founded by Dracula in 1461. The monastery was destroyed and rebuilt in 1589, and thus it is unlikely that Dracula's grave will ever be found.

Dracula's lineage did not die out after his death, and even today it still exists in a high profile family. Two of Dracula's sons had descendants who are ancestors of Queen Elizabeth II. In addition to this, a descendant of Dracula was a woman called Princess Victoria Mary of Teck. She was born in England in 1867 but was actually a Princess of the German Kingdom of Württemberg. In 1893 she married Prince George, the Duke of York. In 1911 she was crowned Queen Mary at the Coronation of her husband, thereafter King George V.

In October 2011 Prince Charles, who owns a home in Transylvania, made a joke about his genealogy when he was involved in an event aimed at raising awareness of the preservation of Transylvania's forests, stating that not only could he prove that he was descended from Dracula, but when making reference to his Transylvanian home he stated, 'So I have a bit of a stake in the country!'

It is unclear why Bram Stoker chose this fifteenth-century Romanian prince as the model for his fictional vampire. Stoker was friends with a Hungarian professor from Budapest, and many have suggested that Dracula might have been further discussed with this friend following Stoker's original discovery of Vlad Tepes in the Whitby library. The cruel history of Vlad the Impaler would have readily loaned itself to Stoker's purposes and would have provided an inspiring villain who needed no fictional back story. Dracula, the Vampire, was a remorseless, cruel being, much like Vlad Tepes. In addition, the events of Dracula's life were played out in a region of the world that was still basically medieval even in Stoker's time. The Balkans had only recently shaken off Turkish rule and influence when Stoker started working on his novel, and the superstitions of the Dark Ages were still prevalent. Transylvania had long been a part of the Austro-Hungarian Empire, but it too had endured a long period of Turkish domination and its culture was still largely medieval.

The legend of the vampire was and still is deeply rooted in that region. There have always been vampire-like creatures in the mythologies of many cultures. However, the vampire, as he became known in Europe, largely originated in the Slavic and Greek lands of Eastern Europe. A supposed epidemic of vampirism swept through Eastern Europe beginning in the late seventeenth century and continuing through the eighteenth century. The number of reported cases rose dramatically in Hungary and the Balkans. From the Balkans the plague spread westward into Germany, Italy, France, England and Spain. Travellers returning from these areas brought with them tales of the undead, igniting an interest in myth of the vampire that has continued to this day. Philosophers in the West began to study the phenomenon. It was during this period that Dom Augustin Calmet wrote his famous treatise on vampirism in Hungary and authors and playwrights first began to explore the vampire myth. Stoker's novel, it could be argued, was merely the result of a long series of works that were inspired by the reports coming from the Balkans and Hungary.

Given the history of the vampire myth in Europe it is perhaps natural that Stoker should place his great vampire fiction in the heart of the region that gave birth to the original myth. Once Stoker had determined on a locality, Vlad Tepes, or Dracula, would stand out as one of the most notorious rulers of the selected region. He was obscure enough that few would recognise the name and those who did would know him for his acts of brutal cruelty; Dracula was a natural candidate for the villain of the novel.

The vampire myth is still widespread in Eastern Europe and the name of Dracula is still remembered in Romanian folklore, but that is the end of any connection between Dracula and the vampire myth in folklore. Outside of

Stoker's novel, the name of Dracula was never linked with the myth of the vampire. Despite his inhuman cruelty, in Romania Dracula is remembered as a national hero who resisted the Turkish conquerors and asserted Romanian national sovereignty against the powerful Hungarian kingdom; but in spite of this, the link between this great hero and the world's most famous vampire are so intertwined that even the Romanian tourist industry plays up to their own Dracula connections in much the same way as you will see in Whitby.

Characteristics of a Vampire

There are – depending upon who you read, or which films you watch – certain characteristics of vampires that determine what they can and can't do. Some of these traits are well known and some have been adapted by authors to suit the needs of their own protagonist. This chapter looks at how to identify a vampire, what can be used to protect against one, and how to destroy a vampire. Bram Stoker, when writing *Dracula*, incorporated many of the folkloric characteristics of the vampire, as will be seen, but he also created some further characteristics for the sake of a good story that have, in the fullness of time, become regarded as definitive vampire characteristics.

From a historical point of view, vampires, in one shape or another, have been around since time immemorial. Early cultures, especially those in Sumeria and South Eastern Europe, had vampire-like demons. These entities were the reanimated corpses of suicides, witches, or evil people. It is not until the early eighteenth century that the term 'vampire' found its way into popular usage following the account of the Serbian soldier, Arnold Paole.

Paole claimed to have been attacked by a vampire whilst he was in Turkish Serbia and had tried to prevent himself from becoming one of the undead by eating some earth from the vampire's grave and covering his body with the vampire's blood. According to legend, Paole was later to die suddenly in a fall from a hay wagon and was buried, only to rise from the grave a month or so later. A number of people claimed to have been attacked by Paole and his body was subsequently exhumed, staked through the heart and burnt.

This story obviously had a massive impact on writers at the time and, in 1819, John Polidori wrote his novella *The Vampyre*, which went on to inspire stories such as *Varney the Vampire* and, ultimately, *Dracula*. It was during this time that the appearance of the vampire took a massive step away from that of the folkloric undead and became the sophisticated and attractive creature of popular fiction. The vampire was a sexually attractive nobleman who committed evil deeds for their own pleasure – the archetypal Gothic Villain. Count Dracula was buying properties in London to enable him to spread vampirism throughout England. He certainly wasn't a tragic and anguished victim, cursed to wander the Earth; he did what he did because he enjoyed it!

According to legend, vampires were described as being bloated with dark ruddy skin. They would sometimes be found with blood streaming from their mouths and noses, a sign taken to be an indication that they had recently feasted on blood. The vampire would often be reported to show signs that its hair, nails, and teeth had grown.

These characteristics were taken to be an indication that the corpse was a vampire but it was more likely that an ignorance of the decomposition process had led to such fears. When a corpse begins to decompose, gases are produced within the body and the resulting pressure within the corpse forces blood out of the mouth and nose, giving the appearance that the body has recently gorged itself on blood. Other reports of the destruction of a vampire mention how the creature groans as it is staked. If a swollen decomposing body was pierced with a stake it is highly likely that the escape of trapped gases would create such a sound. It is also known that, after death, the body's skin and gums lose fluid and contract. This leads to the root of hair, fingernails and teeth being exposed, giving the impression that post-mortem growth has taken place.

To identify a vampire, there were several tests that could be adopted that would be useful indicators that a vampire was about. These include the death of relatives and livestock. The vampire would return to locations that were familiar to them and feed on those that would, in their grief, probably be mentally weaker and less able to resist the vampire's visit. Should the family of the suspected vampire begin to die then a vampire hunter should check the grave. If a large hole is present next to the grave marker then this is a further indicator. To fully confirm whether there is a vampire resting within that grave then a further test should be undertaken.

The final test involves walking a white horse to the grave. If the animal refuses to cross the grave then, it was believed, that is conclusive proof that there is a vampire present.

In order to protect oneself from vampires a number of methods could be employed. These included plants like garlic (as used by Van Helsing), wild rose, or hawthorn; sacred items such as a crucifix, the Host (again used by Van Helsing) and Holy Water (although there is no reference to sacred items from other religions being used to repel vampires this method could have been described more as a means of reinforcing Christian faith than warding off the undead). A vampire would be powerless to enter a house that was protected with these items.

It is interesting to note that garlic is considered as a means of warding off vampires. Some have thought that it is the pungent smell of garlic that manages to repel vampires. A far more likely explanation is that since ancient times, garlic has been used as a healing agent as it helps cleanse the blood and has since acquired a reputation for being a magical plant.

Since a vampire's bite contaminated its victim's blood then garlic could counteract the effect, hence the wearing of garlic around the neck and the placing of it around doors and windows. Also, any vampire that was destroyed might have its body stuffed with garlic to help cleanse the contaminated blood that remained within the corpse.

It was also thought that a vampire would not be able to cross the threshold of a house until invited. Once this invitation had been made, a vampire would be able to enter the house on as many occasions as they wished.

A vampire could be detected by using a mirror, as it would not cast a reflection. This attribute was used by Bram Stoker in *Dracula* when he surprises Jonathan Harker in his room at Castle Dracula, and has found its way into popular vampire culture. Vampires, contrary to popular belief, were not destroyed by exposure to sunlight, and could roam freely, although they were more active during the night. This was seen not only in *Dracula* but also in *Carmilla* by J. S. Le Fanu, where the female vampire would, to all outward appearances, behave like a normal human being.

Vampires were feared beings with supernatural powers but it wasn't until *Dracula* that the belief that a vampire could take the form of a bat, a black dog, or even a ghostly mist became widespread. Dracula, as a vampire, became more sinister by his ability to change his form into that of a giant bat, which allowed him to reach the guest house window and feed on the blood of Lucy Westenra.

The most popular way of destroying a vampire was to stake them through the heart, although in some cultures the mouth or stomach was preferred. Decapitation was also favoured as it was believed to speed up the soul's departure from the body, with the head being located between the corpse's legs or, in some cases, in a totally different grave.

There are records of vampires having been pinned to their graves with iron nails or hawthorn stakes and, in a rare find in Venice in 2006, the skeleton of a woman was found with a brick jammed in her jaws. Archaeologists believe that this was to prevent her from feeding on victims of a plague in the sixteenth century, as it was thought, at that time, that vampires were responsible for spreading plague.

In *Dracula*, Bram Stoker described the vampires as destroyed by being staked in the first instance, then decapitated, and finally having garlic stuffed in their mouths. The actual death of Dracula involved the Count being stabbed through the heart with a knife wielded by Quincey Morris, and his throat slashed by Jonathan Harker before the body crumbled to dust. This death was different from that of the other vampires in the story (namely Lucy and the 'Vampire Brides') in that following his death, Dracula disintegrated. This was a departure from the folkloric death of a vampire and can probably be explained following the discovery of the original manuscript, which revealed a much more dramatic ending …

Mina Harker wrote, on the 6 November:

> *The castle of Dracula now stood out against the red sun and every stone of its*
> *broken battlements was articulated against the light of the setting sun.*

This is where the published version ended, but it was supposed to continue:

> *As we looked there came a terrible convulsion of the earth so that we seemed*
> *to rock to and fro and fell to our knees. At the same moment, with a roar that*
> *seemed to shake the very heavens, the whole castle and the rock and even*
> *the hill on which it stood seemed to rise into the air and scatter in fragments*
> *while a mighty cloud of black and yellow smoke, volume on volume, in rolling*
> *grandeur, was shot upwards with inconceivable rapidity. Then there was a*
> *stillness in nature as the echoes of that thunderous report seemed to come*
> *with the hollow boom of a thunder-clap – the long reverberating roll which*
> *seems as though the floors of heaven shook. Then, down in a mighty ruin*
> *falling whence they rose came the fragments that had been tossed skyward in*
> *the cataclysm ...*

This was a more sensational ending for the book's villain, which was obviously
what Stoker wanted. His original Hollywood-style destruction of Castle
Dracula was to show to the reader that Dracula was something much more
supernatural than a reanimated corpse. Such was the effect of the destruction
of the Count that it became established within vampire mythology that, when
a vampire is 'killed' it will turn to dust.

Vampire writers will, however, decide for themselves what powers best suit
their own protagonists, and as time goes on, the list of attributes will no doubt
continue to grow.

Dracula in Popular Culture

Without a doubt, Count Dracula is the most famous horror character of all time. He has been played by more actors in film and television adaptations than any other. We are all familiar with the 'Big Three', the actors who have typified Dracula throughout the twentieth century: Bela Lugosi, Christopher Lee, and Gary Oldman. However, how many people knew that Dracula was portrayed by John Carradine, Denholm Elliott, Klaus Kinski, Jack Palance, Rutger Hauer, George Hamilton, and Gerard Butler to name but a few. Indeed, it would probably take a page of this book to list all of the actors.

More than 200 films have been made about Dracula and a staggering 649 films have a reference to him. Of those films only a tiny handful mention Whitby or have any resemblance to the actual story. Often the characters are the areas where the greatest changes occur. Dracula, Jonathan and Mina, Van Helsing and Seward are always present. Arthur Holmwood and Quincey Morris are often left out of the story and Lucy is either combined with the character of Mina or has her role reversed with Mina.

It's not just the films and television that have made Dracula the popular character that he is today. He has also made appearances on stage, radio, books, games, comics, cartoons, and even in dance. Since most people are familiar with *Dracula* through film we shall start by exploring that genre first, and we will start with the most famous unofficial Dracula movie, *Nosferatu*.

Nosferatu is often thought to be the first film about Dracula, but it was preceded two years previously by a Hungarian film about Vlad Dracula. However, since no copies remain of that film it is impossible to determine whether the film was about Count Dracula or Vlad Tepes. In 1922, the silent film maker F. W. Murnau was tasked by Prana Films to direct their first (and ultimately only) film, which was inspired both by Bram Stoker's 1897 novel and the wartime experience of Prana Film's Albin Grau, who in 1916 met a Serbian farmer who claimed that his father was one of the Undead.

Nosferatu: Eine Symphonie des Grauens, is very similar to most films about Dracula in that it retains the core characters of Jonathan and Mina Harker, Dracula, Van Helsing and Renfield. The film omits many of the secondary players, such as Holmwood and Morris. This may well have been an influencing factor on later films that also omitted the secondary characters in showing that the story could still be told without the need for extra characters. *Nosferatu*, although including the main characters, did change all of their names and changed the setting from Britain in the 1890s to Germany in 1838. But this is understandable as Prana Films were unable to obtain the filming rights to *Dracula* and needed to make an effort, albeit a token attempt, to disguise the origins of their story.

Nosferatu differed from *Dracula* in that the vampire (called Orlok in the film) does not create other vampires, but kills his victims, causing the inhabitants of the town to blame the plague, which is currently ravaging the town. Also, Orlok must sleep by day, as sunlight would kill him, while Dracula can move about in sunlight. The ending is also substantially different from that of *Dracula* when Orlok is ultimately destroyed at sunrise when the 'Mina' character sacrifices herself to him by keeping him in her room until the sun's rays hit him and cause him to disappear forever.

Again, we can see the influence that *Nosferatu* had on other films in that it created the first cinematic vampire rule; that these monsters must remain in their graves at day and away from sunlight which, as was demonstrated, has a destructive effect on vampires.

Orlok was played by the German actor Max Shreck (whose name translates roughly as 'terror' in German) who played the vampire as a creature of utter repellence. The vampire was completely bald with rat like teeth, pointed malformed ears, a long pointed nose and spindly claw-like fingers. This was a far cry from the description of Dracula provided by Stoker. However, it was such a lasting image that it went on to provide the inspiration for many later cinematic and television vampires, most notably the character of Kurt Barlow in the 1979 television miniseries *Salem's Lot*.

Nosferatu was a success upon its release, but a short-lived one. Florence Stoker, Bram's widow, was unaware of the release of *Nosferatu* and it wasn't until she received an anonymous letter from Berlin that she heard of a film that was 'freely adapted from Bram Stoker's Dracula'. Florence was in financial difficulty and immediately began a legal fight with Prana films claiming copyright infringement. She demanded financial returns from the filmmakers as well as the destruction of all prints and negatives of the film. To avoid paying out, Prana Films declared bankruptcy and Florence could only be satisfied in the court's decision that agreed that copyright had been infringed and ordered the film to be destroyed. However, this vampire film refused to die and a bootleg copy surfaced a few years later and showings resumed in around 1929.

A friend and neighbour of Bram and Florence Stoker who had also worked in the Henry Irving Company in 1899 was Hamilton Deane. He had seen the potential of *Dracula* as a stage play even when Stoker himself had abandoned the idea. Deane, after Bram Stoker's death, sought permission from Florence to adapt the story into a play and this was granted.

It was Hamilton Deane who created the urbane image of Dracula as dressed in white tie and tails with a flowing cape with a stand-up collar. He wanted to portray the Count as someone who could, quite easily, move about in (then) modern society. Deane also made much publicity of the fact that he had employed a nurse at all of his showings who would be in a position to administer help should anyone faint with fright!

The play premiered in 1924 and three years later it crossed the Atlantic where it became a Broadway success. For American audiences the role of Count Dracula was taken by a little-known Hungarian actor called Bela Lugosi.

Also in America, film producer Carl Laemmle Jr had seen the potential in bringing Dracula to a wider audience. Not wanting to make the same mistakes that F. W. Murnau had, he legally obtained the film rights for Dracula and set about a process to bring the Count to the big screen. However, America was gripped by the Great Depression and Laemmle's lavish ideas had to be abandoned.

Having had to abandon his own storyline, Laemmle turned to the Hamilton Deane play (rewritten for American audiences by John Balderston) and the production was soon up and running. However, Laemmle was not keen on using Lugosi in his film version and looked to cast other actors in the role of

Bela Lugosi – the Hungarian actor who made the character of Dracula an international success.

Count Dracula. The search continued in vain and the stage play continued to tour until it reached Los Angeles. Casting was still taking place for the film and Lugosi tried out for the film, in spite of Laemmle's misgivings. Lugosi's persistence (and agreement to be paid a miserly $500 a week) paid off and he reprised his role.

The film was made in 1931, directed by Tod Browning. It was an immediate hit and subsequently became one of the most famous film versions of the story ever as well as reinforcing the image of Dracula as a suave lounge lizard in his white tie, tails and cape and exotic accent; an image so strong that most vampire Halloween costumes follow this cue.

So, Lugosi was Dracula and he became something of a household name and was cast in many more horror movies. Surprisingly, Lugosi only played Dracula on screen twice, his second appearance being in the 1948 comedy *Abbott and Costello Meet Frankenstein,* in which Count Dracula, now the proud owner of Frankensten's monster, seeks to replace the creature's brain. Cue Abbott and Costello.

Lugosi did play the vampire roles in many films and they were Dracula in all but name but it was the 1931 film that set the benchmark for all other films to follow. Sadly, Bela Lugosi died on 16 August 1956 of a heart attack and was buried wearing his famous Dracula cape. He never escaped from the typecasting that was the product of his success.

From 1931 to 1948, Universal Studios made six Dracula films with Lon Chaney Jr and John Carradine playing the part of Count Dracula in several spin-offs. It would be another ten years before the Count would return to the big screen in as memorable an appearance as he had in 1931.

Hammer Film Productions was formed in 1934 by William Hinds and produced several films including, in 1936, a film entitled *The Mystery of the Marie Celeste* starring none other than Bela Lugosi. After several ups and downs such as bankruptcy and the outbreak of the Second World War, Hammer rose from the ashes and continued to make great films.

In 1955 Hammer took its first brave steps into the arena of horror movies and sealed its fate as the leading studio for horror. Their first film was *The Quatermass Experiment,* based on the BBC serial and from then on there was no looking back. In 1957 Hammer produced *The Curse of Frankenstein,* very loosely based on Mary Shelley's masterpiece.

The Curse of Frankenstein was a worldwide success and the fact that it was filmed in colour meant that the horror was more evident on screen than it had ever been before. It is fair to say that the success of the film was a collaboration of a great script by the late Jimmy Sangster and the performance of two actors who were soon to become household names; Peter Cushing and Christopher Lee. The success of *The Curse of Frankenstein* showed the world one thing; the horror genre was still big business! And there was only one name that could draw the audiences into the cinemas. That name was, of course, Dracula.

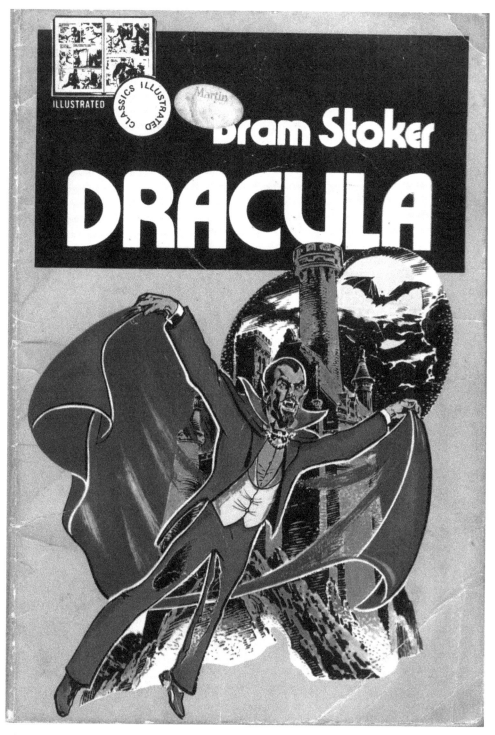

The book that started it all for me. My copy of the *Classics Illustrated* graphic novel: *Dracula* bought for me when I was a young boy.

In 1958 Hammer Films produced their own version of Bram Stoker's novel. The film departed massively from the source although it did keep many of the characters. Jonathan Harker was now a vampire hunter rather than a solicitor and the story begins when he visits Castle Dracula with the intention of killing the Count. Harker fails in his task and is transformed into a vampire himself, only to be destroyed by Van Helsing. Dracula then transforms Harker's fiancée, Lucy Holmwood, into a vampire and Van Helsing and Arthur Holmwood have to destroy the vampire Lucy. Dracula then attacks Mina (Holmwood's wife) before he is tracked down to Castle Dracula and eventually killed by Van Helsing who bathes the Count in sunlight after ripping down some curtains.

Although this film was based in Germany and made no mention of Whitby, it was still an important film in returning the story of Dracula to the front of public consciousness. The success was such that Hammer could not help but create several more films about Dracula. In 1960 they released *Brides of Dracula,* which reinforced the female vampire character within the genre but the public wanted Dracula!

Six years later Christopher Lee brought Dracula back from the grave in *Dracula: Prince of Darkness*. Following this Christopher Lee played Dracula in five more Hammer films, culminating with *The Satanic Rites of Dracula*. By this time Dracula had become a sinister villain of the sort found in James Bond films as he attempts to dominate the world using a bacterial research programme. Lee decided that enough was enough and hung up his cape and fangs.

Throughout Hammer's run of Dracula films other productions were being released that tried to be faithful, at least in part, to the original novel. In 1968 a television adaptation of *Dracula*, starring Denholm Elliott as Count Dracula was released. Although not quite as faithful as it could have been, this film was the first to feature Whitby as a location. This was followed five years later by another television adaptation which featured an unlikely Jack Palance as Count Dracula. This version of the story was also set in Whitby, although the town itself was not a filming location. In an ending, not unlike the 1958 Hammer film, Dracula is cornered in what appears to be a large ballroom and is subdued when sunlight bursts through a window once the curtains have been removed. At this point Van Helsing uses a long spear to stake the Count's heart.

Whitby was to appear in yet another television adaptation of *Dracula*, this time in the 1977 BBC production starring Louis Jordan. This telling was, and still is, the most faithful to the novel. This time not only is the story set in Whitby but it was also filmed in Whitby. Some of the most memorable shots are of the graveyard on the top of the East Cliff where Mina and Lucy walk and rest at their favourite spot. Although the film is a little dated, and the special effects are not up to the expectations of what would be expected by today's standards, the film is definitely one of the best in terms of faithfulness.

It is interesting to note that the three productions that all featured Whitby at this time were television adaptations. The reason that the film productions didn't use or refer to the town is probably down to the simple fact that Whitby was not as well known as it is today. To set a major horror story in a quiet, unknown corner of Yorkshire wouldn't have that immediate link to the audience. The public needed to feel scared, needed to feel that they might possibly become Dracula's next victim, to be worried that a vampire from the depths of Eastern Europe could enter freely one of their large cities and begin to seek victims. When a film studio puts up a large sum of money they want to be sure that the audience are going to identify with the story and recognise the locations. As such, Whitby – then a relatively unknown fishing town – fails to get a mention. With a television adaptation the risks to the financiers are not present to the same extent and the producers can afford to take a few risks and experiment a little.

My mother was born and lived in Whitby and my father also used to spend holidays in Whitby and neither can remember *Dracula* and Whitby being as inextricably linked as they are today when they were younger. Three television adaptations start to show to the public that Dracula is somehow connected to Whitby, sowing the seed of imagination. Then, in 1979, Dracula and Whitby were about to get their biggest exposure yet.

Set entirely in Whitby in 1913, the 1979 film *Dracula* by John Badham was based on the Hamilton Deane and John Balderstone play and featured Frank Langella as the Count. Although this film was set in Whitby it was actually filmed mostly in Cornwall and I suppose this might explain why I was so absorbed by *Dracula*. In 1981 I moved to Cornwall, as my father was in the Royal Navy and my family travelled around a great deal. Shortly after moving to Cornwall I had the hospital stay that I mentioned earlier in the book and my mother gave me the *Classics Illustrated* version of *Dracula*. And, as I mentioned earlier, around this time we would often travel to the picturesque Carlyon Bay on Cornwall's south coast where my sister and I would play on what looked like an old shipwreck, half buried in the sand. It turns out that the shipwreck was, in fact, the set of the *Demeter* from the John Badham film. In 1983 I returned home after a trip to the seaside to discover that on the television that evening was the Badham *Dracula* film. Over the years I managed to visit most of the main locations from that film and it will come as no surprise that this film is still my favourite. It might not be the most accurate to the source novel but it was the film that stuck in my mind and fuelled my imagination.

Dracula benefitted from a fantastic cast that included Donald Pleasance and Laurence Olivier and featured some extremely frightening scenes such as Van Helsing's journey into the old mine to destroy his daughter, Mina, who had become a vampire. However, the film did not perform as well as the filmmakers had hoped, probably due to it having been released in the same year as the comedy Dracula film *Love at First Bite*, which was a critical success and well

Another view of the graveyard that Lucy and Mina were so fond of.

A graveyard at Robin Hood's Bay showing the eerie, yet captivating atmosphere of the Whitby area – something that would have undoubtedly inspired Bram Stoker.

received by audiences, and the artistic *Nosferatu the Vampyre* by Werner Herzog. Badham's *Dracula* seemed to occupy a middle ground between the two films and, sadly, suffered critically as a result.

However, all was not lost! As mentioned, the Badham film was the first cinematic *Dracula* to feature Whitby as a major location and this film, coupled with the earlier television adaptations, catapulted Whitby onto the world stage as the link between *Dracula* and Whitby had been established.

Sometime in the early 1980s a small photographic shop on Marine Parade in Whitby was bought and turned into a tourist attraction calling itself 'The Dracula Experience'. It was, and still is, an excellent attraction in which the visitor walks through various scenes from the story, assisted by cloaked figures lurking within the shadows.

At about the same time the Town Crier at the time was a man called Rex Greenwood. In addition to his Town Crying duties he also used to dress as Dracula and take people on tours around the town, pointing out locations from the story. Rex also ran a Dracula Fan Club which, I am proud to say, I was a member of. Sadly, Rex died in 2004 but without his enthusiasm, I doubt whether the link between Whitby and Dracula would have been as strong as it is today.

Throughout the 1980s Whitby built on its connection with *Dracula* and many tourists would make their way to the town to see the locations mentioned in the book, but it wasn't until 1992 when another film was produced that was, without doubt, the most successful and widely accepted *Dracula* film of all time, and it was because of this that Whitby and *Dracula* became inseparable. The irony of this event was that this film did not mention Whitby at all!

Francis Ford Coppola had made his name with many great films such as *Apocalypse Now*, *The Godfather*, and *Peggy Sue Got Married* and if it hadn't been for such a successful resume, and an excellent script by James V. Hart that followed the original novel quite closely, then it is doubtful that *Bram Stoker's Dracula* would ever had been made as it was the opinion of most film studios that Dracula had been done to death and therefore not worth the investment.

The film, *Bram Stoker's Dracula*, begins in 1462 and was unique in that it was the first film to link Vlad the Impaler with the fictional Count Dracula. In the opening sequence Dracula is distraught following the suicide of his wife that he renounces God and vows to rise from the grave. The film moves to Victorian England and from here on it does a good job of sticking fairly close to the original novel. A sub-story not featured in the book is that Mina looks exactly like Dracula's long dead wife and a love affair begins between Mina and Dracula. All the characters from the book are present, including the often missed Quincey Morris, but sadly the story does not mention Whitby.

Upon its release *Bram Stoker's Dracula* was a critical success and received many favourable reviews from critics worldwide. *Dracula* had been reinvented and was no longer the stereotypical character that he had become through decades of *Dracula* spin-off films.

In Whitby, the release of the 1992 film prompted a face lift for the Dracula Experience building and it was redecorated with features from that film such as wolf's head sculptures and a full-sized mannequin of Count Dracula. Even the sign writing was changed to match the font of the film's poster.

Dracula was firmly back in the public consciousness and was no longer a low-budget film character. People were now reading the original novel and Whitby's connections with *Dracula* were more widely known.

Following *Bram Stoker's Dracula* filmmakers began to experiment again with stories about the Count, which included such adventures as *The Killer Barbys vs. Dracula* (Dracula is awoken by the Killer Barbys' new song), *Dracula 3000* (which sees the Count infiltrate a space ship and start killing the passengers), the animated film *The Batman vs. Dracula*, and many more. Many of these films appeared to be a throwback to the B-Movie era and, although not faithful retellings of the Dracula story, they did prove that Dracula was, once again, big business.

Following on from *Bram Stoker's Dracula* the world saw an increase in the interest of vampires and the stories of Anne Rice were developed into films, the most successful being, without a doubt, *Interview with the Vampire*. Quentin Tarantino wrote and starred in *From Dusk 'Til Dawn* which featured two fugitives and their hostages fighting for their lives in a Mexican bar run by vampires. Long-running television and film sagas began to emerge such as *Buffy the Vampire Slayer*, and the *Twilight* series, which featured vampires who were on the side of good as well as those who were evil. Vampires were back!

The Dracula phenomenon wasn't limited to films; many books were also produced featuring the Count which explored further the character outside of the Bram Stoker story. Some of the books tried to expand on Stoker's novel and were created as sequels. Probably the best of these sequels is Freda Warrington's *Dracula the Undead*, which reunites the characters from the original novel as they revisit Transylvania and later discover that Dracula has risen again. This story also develops the Dracula–Mina love story that became popular after the Coppola film.

Dracula has not been limited to stage, film, and the written word. The National Ballet Theatre premiered their version of *Dracula* in 1997 and it has toured the world since then, proving to be a highly popular and successful show.

In addition to the performing arts, Dracula has appeared in many computer games. Some feature a character which bears a passing resemblance to Dracula; others feature the Count as a main character. I can particularly recommend the series of adventure games: *Dracula: Resurrection, Dracula: The Last Sanctuary* and *Dracula 3 – The Path of the Dragon*. These games take place after Stoker's novel and feature the continuing fight against Dracula.

Stoker wrote to make money – that much is clear – but he did not live to see the commercial success that followed the publication of *Dracula*. Vampire stories and films have been big business throughout the twentieth century and into the twenty-first century and will probably continue to entertain for a long time to come. This is the legacy left by Bram Stoker, and it probably would not have happened if he hadn't taken his summer holiday in Whitby in 1890.

Bram Stoker:
A Short Biography

We are in Dublin's north side and it is 8 November 1847. A young boy is born to Abraham Stoker and Charlotte Thornley at their home, 15 Marino Crescent, Clontarf. He is the third of seven children and one day he will create the world's most famous vampire.

Illness kept him virtually bedridden until the age of seven. Although he remained shy throughout his life, in his adolescence Bram Stoker was anything but sickly and became a formidable athlete, being crowned University Athlete at Trinity College, Dublin.

Several publications were to influence Stoker during the nineteenth century and it was these horror stories that were to help him create the character of Dracula.

One night in June 1816, on the banks of Lake Geneva, a group of friends had settled down for a night of entertainment. The group read aloud from the *Tales of the Dead*, a collection of horror tales, and at the end one of the group, Lord Byron, suggested that they each write a ghost story. Byron's friend, Percy Bysshe Shelley, wrote *A Fragment of a Ghost Story* and five further ghost stories, which were published posthumously as *The Journal at Geneva (including ghost stories) and on return to England, 1816*. His wife, Mary Shelley, worked on a fantastic tale that would later evolve into *Frankenstein*. Lord Byron wrote (and quickly abandoned) the embryo of a story called *Fragment of a Novel*.

Also within this group was Byron's physician, John Polidori, who took Byron's aborted story and used it as the basis for his own tale, *The Vampyre*, the first vampire story published in English.

Dismissed by Byron, Polidori travelled through Italy before returning to England. His story, *The Vampyre*, which featured the main character Lord Ruthven, was published in the April 1819 issue of *New Monthly Magazine*

An illustration from J. S. Le Fanu's *Carmilla*.

without Polidori's permission and, frustratingly, was released as a new work by Byron.

In addition to these great stories, the popular *Penny Dreadfuls* (a series of horror stories that cost only a penny) were dominated by J. Rhymer's epic horror tale, *Varney the Vampire*, which began in 1845 and was published as a huge novel of 220 chapters in 1847.

Varney the Vampire introduced many of the vampire characteristics that would later influence Stoker. Varney had fangs, left two puncture wounds on the neck and was of incredible strength. These characteristics would become familiar as the traits of a vampire from then on. However, unlike modern vampire tales, but entirely in keeping with the current trend, Varney the Vampire was able to move about in the daylight. As we shall now see, this was used by another author whose work would have undoubtedly have influenced Stoker. The vampire story was big business and many authors were penning their own works.

J. Sheridan Le Fanu had also recently written his famous and haunting vampire novel, *Carmilla*. Set in Styria (a state in the south-east of Austria), it tells the story of a young girl called Laura who befriends and becomes romantically involved with the mysterious Carmilla, who, unbeknown to Laura, is the vampire Mircalla Karnstein. Many features of Stoker's novel have parallels with *Carmilla*, such as the original location for *Dracula*, issues of sleepwalking, and the inclusion of an 'expert' in the way of the vampire.

Bram Stoker.

Stoker had written a short story that was not published until his death, called *Dracula's Guest*. Believed by many to be a first chapter to *Dracula*, it was released in 1914 in the book *Dracula's Guest and other Weird Stories* by Stoker's widow who stated:

> *To his original list of stories in this book, I have added an hitherto unpublished episode from Dracula. It was originally excised owing to the length of the book, and may prove of interest to the many readers of what is considered my husband's most remarkable work.*

Both *Dracula's Guest* and *Carmilla* are told in the first person and feature the tomb of a mysterious noblewoman. But Le Fanu's influence did not stop there. We have seen earlier how Stoker took fellow holidaymakers from Whitby and transformed them into Mrs Westenra, Lucy Westenra, and Mina Murray but he also took inspiration from the description of Carmilla when creating the character of Lucy. They are tall, slim and beautiful, with large eyes and full lips. They were both sleepwalkers, although in Lucy's case it was her sleepwalking that would ultimately lead to her demise. The close friendship between Laura and Carmilla could also have led, in some part, to the creation of the characters of Lucy and Mina.

Doctor Abraham Van Helsing also owes a debt to characters in *Carmilla* and elsewhere. In Le Fanu's story we are presented with vampire expert Baron Vordenburg who helps investigate and vanquish the vampire. In addition, the story itself is presented as part of a casebook belonging to an occult doctor called Hesselius. It doesn't take much imagination to note the small similarity in the two names. The creation of Van Helsing is not just limited to elements of *Carmilla*. It has been suggested that the surname may have been influenced by the Danish town that is home to Hamlet's castle – namely, Helsingor. Does the name owe something to the ancient alchemist Van Helmont, from T. J. Pettigrew's 1844 book on superstitions. Maybe it is a blend of all three, but what is certain is that the name Bram is a shortened version of Abraham. This

The cover of *Dracula's Guest*. Published after Bram Stoker's death

The cover of *Varney the Vampire* – a major influence on Stoker's work.

Joseph Sheridan Le Fanu – author of *Carmilla*.

indicates a certain identification with the main hero of the story and it is very likely that many of Van Helsing's character traits were shared by Stoker.

It is also interesting to note that Stoker's father worked with J. Sheridan Le Fanu's brother, William Richard Le Fanu, at Dublin Castle, and later in life Stoker himself would share the office next door to W. R. Le Fanu's son. It is with little surprise following this sort of exposure, to find that *Dracula* was inspired in part by the story *Carmilla*.

Stoker's wish was always to become a writer, but his father had different, much safer plans. Stoker was to follow his father into a career as a civil servant at Dublin Castle. While working within the civil service, he wrote a book entitled *Duties of Clerks of Petty Sessions in Ireland*. This book of rules was not published until 1879, by which time Stoker was married, living in another country, and following a new profession.

During his tenure within the civil service, Stoker continued to write stories; the first, a dream fantasy entitled *The Crystal Cup*, was published by the *London Society*. A serialised four-part horror piece entitled *The Chain of Destiny* followed three years later. He also took unpaid positions as theatrical critic for Dublin's *Evening Mail* and later as editor of the *Irish Echo*, in an attempt to indulge his passion for writing.

Stoker idolised the actor Sir Henry Irving, so much so that he would later name his son after him. Stoker had first seen Irving when he was nineteen at the Theatre Royal in Dublin, and it was at this time that Stoker began his work as a volunteer theatre critic. They did not meet until some nine years later.

In 1878, Henry Irving offered Stoker the job of actor/manager of the Lyceum Theatre in London following a favourable review of Irving's performance as Hamlet. With this offer, Stoker resigned from the civil service, married Florence Balcombe and created a new life in London. Florence Balcombe was the daughter of Lieutenant Colonel James Balcombe (who also lived on Marino Crescent) and was considered to be the on-off girlfriend of Oscar Wilde. Stoker and Wilde had been friends as students but when Florence chose to marry Stoker the decision upset and angered Wilde and the friendship disintegrated. For Wilde, things looked up and he became extremely famous and successful until he was tried and convicted for gross indecency with other men. Upon his release from prison, Wilde fled to Paris. Stoker travelled to visit him and the two reformed their friendship. Within a year, Florence had given birth to their only child, Noel, but Stoker and his wife, though continuing to keep up appearances, are believed to have become estranged.

Stoker was immersed in his work, yet despite his heavy professional duties, he found the time to continue to write. His first fiction book, *Under the Sunset*, consisted of eight spooky stories for children. His first full-length novel, *The Snake's Pass*, was published in 1890. That same year was the beginning of Stoker's masterpiece, *Dracula*, which, when published in 1897, was a runaway success.

Stoker's notes, as mentioned earlier, were written on scraps of paper which he would later cobble together. His handwriting was, as he himself admitted, particularly bad and his notes often difficult to decipher. One of these notes, written in March 1890, showed that he'd had the idea for his groundbreaking novel. The note reads:

> *Young man goes out – sees girls one tries – to kiss him not on the lips but throat. Old Count interferes – rage and fury diabolical. This man belongs to me I want him.*

Other notes developed the idea further:

> *Loneliness, the Kiss... 'this man belongs to me I want him'. The visitors – is it a dream – women stoop to kiss him. Terror of death. Suddenly Count turns her away – 'this man belongs to me'; 'Women kissing'; 'Belongs to Me'.*

This shows that Stoker had formulated the aspects of the story that would later make it into the novel, as these were the notes that would make up the section of Dracula where Jonathan Harker realises that the Count is actually a vampire – albeit a vampire who has just saved him from the three vampire brides that live within Castle Dracula.

The notes as written indicate that what Stoker had experienced was a very vivid dream. In fact Stoker used to joke that his inspiration for Dracula came about from a dream following a generous helping of dressed crab.

It is also possible to speculate as to what was on Stoker's mind when he had this dream. Stoker's employer at the time, Sir Henry Irving, was fond of the play Macbeth and the three vampire brides certainly have a connection with the three witches from that play. Stoker's troubled marriage is hinted at by the notes about loneliness and being kissed by the strange women. Likewise, his own idolisation of Sir Henry, as well as Sir Henry's 'ownership' of Stoker, are hinted at with the line, 'This man belongs to me'.

But this was not all that influenced Stoker. He had his nobleman – the Count – as Polidori had his Lord Ruthven. The female vampires (taken from Carmilla perhaps) are targeting the neck in much the same way as Varney the Vampire did.

In August 1890, Bram Stoker travelled to Whitby where he spent a week alone before being joined by his wife and son. During his time in Whitby he worked on gathering notes on local superstition and folklore, chatting to fishermen and coastguards. At that time, my own great-great-grandfather, Richard Smith, was the Chief Coastguard at Whitby, and I often wonder if he spoke with Bram Stoker at this time. It is recorded in Stoker's notes that one coastguard that he did speak with was William Petherick, who told him about the wreck of the Dmitry in 1885. Stoker later turned this wreck into the Demeter.

Stoker visited the library where he found books about local folklore and was inspired by tales of the barguest, which took the form of a great black dog with glowing eyes. Like the wreck of the Dmitry, the barguest was woven into Dracula as the black dog that leaps from the beached ship on Tate Hill Sands.

And there was the book by William Wilkinson that Stoker copied a passage from verbatim. A single passage that marked the creation of the world's most famous horror villain. The note read:

DRACULA in the Wallachian language means Devil. The Wallachians were, at that time, as they are at present, used to give this surname to any person who rendered himself conspicuous either by courage, and actions, or cunning.

When Stoker left Whitby he continued to work on Dracula, developing his notes. In 1893 Stoker took a holiday to Peterhead in Scotland and discovered Slains Castle to the north of Cruden Bay. This great castle was perched on the top of the cliffs and it is widely believed that this was to become the model upon which Castle Dracula would be based.

All in all, Stoker took seven years to write Dracula and the level of research that he conducted to create the story paid off. Stoker never travelled to Transylvania and it is clear to see that out of the whole novel, it is the Whitby sections that are the ones with the most atmosphere.

Although he wrote several short stories, novels and essays, Stoker's name was to be made famous by *Dracula*. Stoker wrote two horror stories that, whilst not gaining the same amount of fame as *Dracula*, still maintain their place in literary history.

In 1903 Stoker published *The Jewel of the Seven Stars*, a tale about an archaeologist's attempts to resurrect a long-dead Egyptian queen. The book was criticised for its gruesome ending and in 1912, when trying to republish it, Stoker was forced to rewrite the ending to give it a much more positive angle. The book was, like *Dracula*, to influence almost every Mummy film that followed. In 2008 *The Jewel of the Seven Stars* was republished to include the original 1903 ending.

In 1911 Stoker published *The Lair of the White Worm*, a book that was probably his next most famous piece of work after Dracula. Once again Stoker drew from local legends to inspire him and loosely based his novel on the legend of the Lambton Worm, a story from the north-east of England about a young man called John Lambton who avoids going to church and goes fishing instead. While fishing he catches a strange looking eel and casts it down a well in disgust. John forgets about the worm and goes off to fight in the Crusades. Whilst away the worm grows and frees itself from the well and terrorises the local community. The worm also has regenerative powers and when it is cut into parts it re-attaches itself.

John returns from the Crusades and vows to destroy the worm. He seeks advice from a witch who tells him to wear armour covered with sharp blades. John does as instructed and faces the worm in the River Wear. As the worm coils itself around John it cuts itself apart on the sharp blades and the pieces drop into the river where they are swept away before they can re-attach themselves, thus destroying the worm.

The Lair of the White Worm is set in Derbyshire and tells the story of the mysterious Lady Arabella March who is guardian to a great white worm (similar to the Lambton Worm) that lives in a pit beneath her house. The hero of the story is Adam Salton who decides to destroy the worm. He achieves this with a stash of dynamite and a bolt of lightning.

Both *The Jewel of the Seven Stars* and *The Lair of the White Worm* were turned into films and much was made of the fact that they were the product of Bram Stoker in publicising them.

Bram Stoker continued to write until his death on 20 April 1912 at 26 St George's Square, London, following a number of strokes. He was cremated at Golders Green and an urn placed in the East Columbarium. In his obituary there was no mention of *Dracula*, a story that has been filmed more times than any other book besides the Bible. He died without ever knowing how influential his creation was to become.

Florence, however, must have known how popular *Dracula* was when she posthumously published *Dracula's Guest*, doubtless to earn some extra money on the back of her husband's famous creation. She was also acutely aware of the financial success of the story when she attempted to sue F. W. Murnau when he made the film *Nosferatu* in 1922, based heavily on her dead husband's novel.

Bram Stoker, the third of seven children, left us a legacy that has formed the very backbone of every vampire film, story and legend created since 1897. When you think of a vampire, you think of Dracula.

Afterword

I closed my last chapter with the assumption that when you think about vampires you will automatically think of Dracula. But when you think of Dracula, you don't automatically think of Whitby.

Throughout this book we have looked at the story of Dracula and how Bram Stoker was inspired by Whitby. We have seen how Dracula was inspired by other works of fiction and by some actual events, but they are simply meat for the bones. The backbone of Dracula is Whitby. Stoker never visited Transylvania but chose to use it as a location after discovering it in a book in the Whitby library. That same book gave him the name 'Dracula', borrowed from Vlad the Impaler. Put simply, without Whitby there would have been no Dracula.

For me, Whitby is a magical place with a history far greater and richer than it first seems. Throughout history Whitby has evolved into a town that has its own traditions, has made its own fortune and has become a popular holiday destination.

Today, thousands of people flock to Whitby and there is no getting away from the legacy left by Bram Stoker. Of course Whitby has other great things to offer but, for me, it will always be Dracula's Whitby.

Bibliography

Akers, Timothy: *Wrecks and Salvage Around the North & East Riding of Yorkshire 1796 to 1896 AD*. Self-published, 2003.

Aughton, Peter: *Endeavour: The Story of Captain Cook's First Great Epic Voyage*. Cassell & Co., London, 2002.

Baignet, Michael; Leigh, Richard & Lincoln, Henry: Holy Blood Holy Grail. Jonathan Cape, London, 2005.

Bartlett, Wayne & Idriceanu: *Legends of Blood: The Vampire in History and Myth*. Sutton Publishing, Stroud 2005.

Belford, Barbara: *Bram Stoker and the Man Who Was Dracula*. Da Capo Press, Cambridge, Mass., 2002.

Davies, Bernard: *Whitby Dracula Trail*. Scarborough Borough Council, Scarborough (Date Unknown).

Dixon, Stephen: 'Why Dracula Never Loses His Bite'. *Irish Times*, 15 August 2009.

Frank, Alan: Monsters and Vampires. Cathay Books, London, 1979.

Frayling, Christopher: *Nightmare – The Birth of Horror*. BBC , London 1996.

Hodkinson, Paul: *Goth: Identity, Style and Subculture*. Berg Publishers Ltd. 2002.

Hughes, William: *Beyond Dracula:Bram Stoker's Fiction and its Cultural Contexts*. MacMillan, Basingstoke 2000.

McNally, Raymond T. and Florescu, Radu: *In Search of Dracula*. Robson Books, London 1997.

Murray, Paul: *From the Shadows of Dracula: A Life of Bram Stoker*. Jonathan Cape Ltd., London 2004.

Pettigrew, Thomas Joseph: *On Superstitions Connected with the History and Nature of Medicine and Surgery*. John Churchill, London 1844.

Stamp, Cordelia: *Dracula Discovered*. Caedmon of Whitby, Whitby 2001.

Stoker, Bram: *Dracula*. Penguin Books, London. 1994.

Summers, Montague: *The Vampire*. Senate, London 1995.

Waters, Colin: *Gothic Whitby*. The History Press, Stroud 2009.

Waters, Colin: *Whitby & The Dracula Connection*. Whitby Press, Whitby.

Whitbysights.co.uk: *A Brief History – Whitby Sights*.

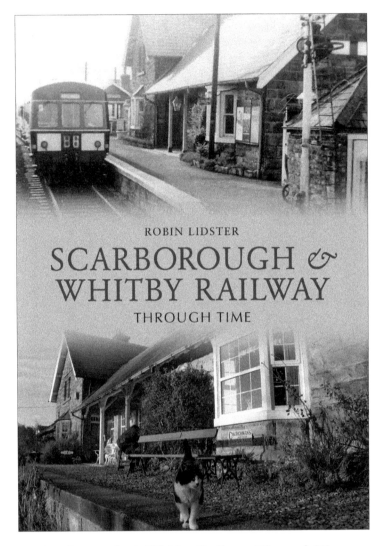

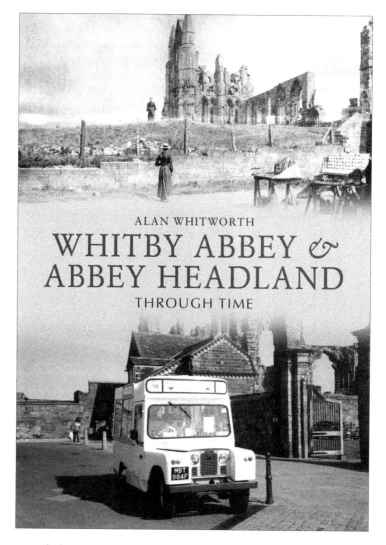

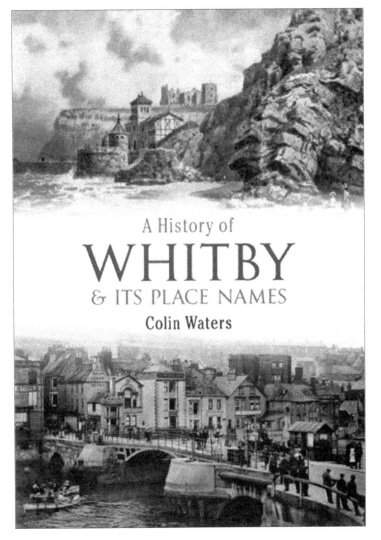

A History of Whitby *&* its Place Names

Colin Waters

This absorbing and well-researched book by local historian Colin Waters is full of fascinating facts presented as an easy to read A–Z. With explanations of the origins of the town's street, village, and place names and how they are linked to people and events in Whitby's history, this book presents a new way of looking at the area's ancient origins.

978 1 4456 0429 9

144 pages